an easy, commonsense approach to revitalizing
your home, business, and relationships

feng shui

back to balance

Sally Fretwell

New World Library
Novato, California

 New World Library
14 Pamaron Way
Novato, California 94949

CIP information available.

ISBN 1-57731-221-X
First printing, February 2002

Printed in Canada on acid-free, partially recycled paper
Distributed to the trade by Publishers Group West

10 9 8 7 6 5 4 3 2 1

Editor
Meg Morris

Copyeditor
Dolores Dwyer

Writing Assistants
Meg Morris, Carol Lamb

Cover Design
Mary Beth Salmon

Text Design
Anne Chesnut

Moose Illustrations
Sally Fretwell

Bring light to living.

I dedicate this book to my children, Pat and Susie, who I get to be goofy and silly with. To my husband who has taught me so much about balance and the principles that guide Feng Shui. To my mom, Susie, and sister Mimi who fly on eagle wings. To my father who taught me to be tenacious, and to my brother Bob who is my guardian angel here on earth.

Special thanks to nine great friends, marvelous Meg, Melissa, Carol, Margaret, Deb, Rae, Char, Audrey and Anne, who have supported me in this endeavor. And finally, thanks to my clients who prompted me to write this book.

Contents

Appendix
Nine Star Ki—
Personal and Celebrity Astrology Charts

When I was twenty years old, I saw Feng Shui in action for the first time. My parents, after retiring, decided to sell the family home and move to our twenty-four-foot-square New Hampshire ski chalet. It was barely large enough for one person, let alone a couple who had very different ideas about what an ideal retirement home would look like.

My father was a businessman who worked long hours even in retirement and spent many hours on the phone. He was perfectly happy working in his basement office of the chalet, which had dark wood paneling. A spiral staircase wound down to what we joked was his "dungeon." My mother was the opposite of my father. She told him she would not live in a square, dark chalet—she wanted a round house. Not wanting to move from his perfect setup, my father suggested she build her own dream house next to his. So, she did. She built a round house connected to the chalet by a bridge.

The house was like a birdhouse with huge, open windows, white stucco walls, and high ceilings. It included her bedroom, a large bathroom, and a living room on the top floor; a kitchen, bathroom, bedroom, and another living area downstairs for guests. She decorated the house with a bright green carpet, Indian totems and fetishes and an old-timers' tub in her bathroom. She was lively, light, and esoteric—the type of person who called on her "parking angel" to find a parking spot. Her house was perfect for her, and she spent many hours painting there.

My parents' homes reflected their personalities and were their ideal sanctuaries. Each house had a kitchen and a bathroom, which allowed them to follow their separate schedules and yet share their lives by meeting for meals together. The bridged entryway had a sunroom area that housed buckets of bread crumbs to feed the wild animals—one of their shared interests. Every day they would talk as they fed the bears and raccoons that visited.

Their example made a deep impression on me: I saw how important homes are to our well-being and our relationships. In my practice of Feng Shui, I often think of my parents' limitless creativity, remembering that there is always a way to create harmonious living and working spaces.

Introduction

Close your eyes and bring yourself to the most beautiful spot you have ever been. Would it be New England in the autumn? Or perhaps the French Alps in the spring? Maybe it would be the flower garden at your grandmother's house? Most of us can think of a spot that brings us into a heart space, and which reminds us of fond, peaceful memories. Why is this place so special? Would you say it has good Feng Shui?

Feng Shui is about balance; it is not about putting a lucky object in your wealth area. It takes universal principles and creates balance by looking with new eyes at all aspects of your life. It requires you to consider your home as an integral part of who you are.

To open your understanding of Feng Shui, begin by taking a walk through your home to see what you have on your walls, notice where the kitchen and bathrooms are located. Ask yourself, How easy is it to move through the house? Does each room have easy access? All of these reflections are significant because your subconscious negotiates this information every day. The practice of Feng Shui guides you to see how your life and home are interlinked. The energy flow through a house is similar to how energy circulates through our bodies. In fact, your home is a buffer zone to the outside world. It is essential that it be balanced and in harmony with your body, mind, and spirit. It is your retreat from the world—the place you recharge after a long day.

Impressions from the world flow through you every day as you walk down a road, go to the supermarket, or sit in your office. The brain is like a computer, registering color, angles, sounds, and even feelings. Your eyes direct the show, labeling the items and categorizing them as you go along—for example, car, house, red, black, person, mother, and so on.

Feng Shui is about being aware of what is going on around you. Seeing is only the tip of the iceberg. The energy or intuition behind Feng Shui is simply tuning into the subtle aspects of an environment. Beyond the sense of sight, touch, sound and smell, we have an innate ability to sense what is around us. Mothers often report the ability to sense where their child is or how he or she is feeling even though their five senses can't tell them this. When I introduce this concept at Feng Shui classes,

I use one of my favorite exercises. I take the class to a museum and ask everyone in the group to close their eyes as I position them in front of an item in the space. Each group member reports an amazing ability to identify some aspect of the item before him or her.

One woman, whom I had positioned in front of a painting of a field of lilies and a house in the background, felt the impression of her grandmother—warm and comforting. She also began to remember the homemade muffins her grandmother would bake on Sundays during her summer visits. When she opened her eyes, she was amazed to see the lilies before her—they were just like those that grew in front of her grandmother's house. The picture depicted the cozy summer scenery she associated with her grandmother. This is one of the many examples I've seen of our innate abilities to sense the unseen.

Feng Shui is about being aware of what is going on around you. Seeing is only the tip of the iceberg. The energy or intuition behind Feng Shui is simply tuning into the subtle aspects of an environment.

When you enter a new space you register the subtle aspects of the environment, including the state of the people in it. For example, we have all been in places that feel stressful. Think of a busy doctor's office where people are racing around as if wearing roller skates. How does your nervous system react to that kind of environment? Are you able to relax? Compare that now to the most comfortable place you know, a place you can completely relax in. Every space can feel that harmonious—whether its main purpose is to create an atmosphere of relaxation, social interaction, or intellectual focus—by creating balance through the use of color, placement, optimum flow, and seeing clearly what is needed from an objective perspective.

Understanding the energetic perspective that guides Feng Shui practices is essential. For example, one of my clients read about putting a crystal between the refrigerator and the stove. She followed the advice without understanding the energetic dynamic behind it. She asked me why the book suggested this "remedy." I replied that the cold from the refrigerator and the heat from the stove counteract each other, causing them not to function at their optimum. Once she understood this, she could have used a number of solutions, from using a piece of wood to separate the appliances to adding a countertop. The "why" behind the practice is the most important and empowering aspect of Feng Shui.

Feng Shui suggestions only work if you feel comfortable with them. Applying your own intuition is best. When I educate clients on the energetic dynamic of a room, they often come up with the best solution. This once played out when I went to a client's house and saw that she had hung a saxophone, flutes, and other musical instruments from the beams over her bed. Every kind of instrument but a drum set greeted her husband and her every night as they looked up from their bed! I laughed, and asked her why she had done it. She said she and her husband had been having a hard time sleeping, so she had consulted a Feng Shui book. It suggested that hanging flutes on the beams would help them sleep better, and she had thought, "The more the better." But it wasn't helping them sleep; in fact, they felt uneasy.

After I explained to her the energetic dynamic behind the flute idea, she came up with her own intuitive solution, which both she and her husband could live with. She decided to create a soft, faux ceiling out of a gauze material. This softened the ceiling and hid the beams, creating a very sensual, nurturing place to sleep. They reported back to me that they were sleeping like babies—and the music store took back the saxophone!

Over the past few years, I've seen an influx of Feng Shui rules for "good" and "bad." Feng Shui is not about simplistic, dualistic thinking; rather, it is a support system like any other modality, which brings light to patterns and strengthens the individual. Feng Shui is a life-enhancing philosophy that is based on balance and self-discovery. To better understand the concept of non-dualistic perspective, consider the following story:

A farmer buys a horse. His neighbor comes over and exclaims how fortunate the farmer is to possess such a magnificent animal. The farmer replies, "Who knows what's good or bad?" Then the horse runs away. The neighbor reappears and commiserates on this great misfortune, only to hear the farmer calmly repeat, "Who knows what's good or bad?" The next day the horse returns and brings with him a drove of wild horses. The neighbor enviously exclaims, "How fortunate you are!" Once again the farmer patiently reiterates, "Who knows what's good or bad?" Again this proves to be wise, for the next day the farmer's son

Feng Shui is a life-enhancing philosophy that is based on BALANCE *and self-discovery.*

tries to mount one of the wild horses and gets thrown, breaking his leg. The neighbor expresses his sympathy and sadly replies, "What a misfortune!" The farmer replies with his familiar unemotional statement. The farmer's logic prevails, for the following day soldiers come to recruit men for battle, and the son is exempted because of his injury.

The moral of this story is that labeling events as "good" or "bad" limits our experiences, as we never can know the entire purpose of all the events of our lives.

Feng Shui, like any other subject, can be interpreted in many ways. How you use Feng Shui depends on how you filter it through your own perception. Many of my clients call me with concerns about conflicting information they've read or been told about Feng Shui, or they are worried about how to apply the different Feng Shui "rules." If information you receive brings you into a fearful place, then it's time to look at it in a different way. If the information makes you feel supported, then it's empowering information. My best advice to them and you is to have fun. That's why I like to call it "Fun Shui."

Feng Shui Astrology, called "Nine Star Ki," helps you determine the energetic dynamic of families and office workers. This system is a profound tool to empower a group as a whole. It allows deeper understanding of why some people naturally work well together and why others do not. It explains why some people feel they have to compromise or struggle in some relationships while others fit like a glove with no effort. My clients enjoy using Nine Star Ki as a guide for learning new ways to feel in rhythm with others and their surroundings. I hope you, too, will find it useful in supporting balance to your living and working spaces, as well as your relationships. The entire Nine Star Ki system is outlined in Chapter 2 and the Appendix of the book.

My hope is that this book will help you engage your mind, body, and spirit in the practice of Feng Shui, and that the real-life stories of how people have improved their lives inspire you to experiment and bring even more peace, joy, and abundance into your life.

The moral of this story is that labeling events as "good" or "bad" limits our experiences, as we never can know the entire purpose of all the events of our lives.

applying **Feng Shui** *to your life*

Perhaps you've read or heard about Feng Shui and want to know how to apply it to your life. Or perhaps you already practice Feng Shui and are looking for a fresh perspective. *Feng Shui: Back to Balance* invites you to use all levels of your being and encourages you to view the practice of Feng Shui and your life in a holistic way—one in which your relationships, life experiences, home, and workspace are interconnected. This book also guides you to use your senses and intuition to discover the energetic dynamics of spaces.

Your intuition

What is intuition? It is your inner knowing. Take, for example, a time when you made a last-minute decision that had no apparent rational reason, yet ended up making your life easier. Whether it was an impulse to take another route while driving, thus avoiding an accident, or to sell a stock option just before its value plummeted—your intuition was at work. It sent you an insight, or a feeling, which some people call a "gut feeling." The more you pay attention to your inner knowing, the more you realize it is active all the time. Being in tune with your intuition allows you to gain clarity and self-assurance. It can be your best and most loyal friend.

Usually your first impressions are your intuition at work. Sometimes your intellect or reasoning powers override your intuition by evaluating and critiquing. If you hear a struggle going on in your head, for example, the reasons why or why not to do something, a guilty or fearful feeling, then more than your intuition is at work. Trusting your inner knowing frees your mind to do what it does best—categorizing and computing information. So let your intuition lead your mind. In other words, if you get an intuitive "hit" on something, trust that it is valuable information.

To explain the concept of intuition and energetic sensitivity to clients, I use one of my favorite workshop exercises. I ask the audience to close their eyes, as I hand out five or six sheets of differently colored paper to a few individuals. Then I ask everyone who isn't holding a sheet of paper to open his or her eyes. One by one I ask those holding the paper with their eyes closed to explain their first impressions. One woman said the sheet of paper I gave her reminded her of sunshine—the page she held was a rich yellow. A man had an aquamarine piece of paper, which reminded him of sailing. The participants who trusted their first impressions usually guessed the correct color.

The exercise above illustrates one of the most basic principles of Feng Shui: Your body, spirit, and emotions respond to unarticulated impressions from your environment. In other words, every object holds a vibration with which you interact. Your body and energetic field

---

Being in tune with your intuition allows you to gain clarity and self-assurance. It can be your best and most loyal friend.

- Your intuition is at work all the time.

- Your senses receive information about your environment— tasting, seeing, touching, hearing, and smelling.

- Your mind computes facts and labels them for referencing.

- The impressions you receive affect you both consciously and unconsciously.

- Everything is filtered through your personal perspective.

register everything you come in contact with—whether you are conscious of it or not. The yellow sheet of paper my student held made an impression on her without her even seeing it. Add to that your hearing, sight, touch, taste, and smell—which pick up color, light, shadow, sound, sense of space or closure, air circulation, mood, old emotions, and texture—and your mind is active, labeling your impressions.

Although Feng Shui offers guidelines to assist in balancing yourself and your environment, it is up to you to trust your intuition and put the nonmental aspects of Feng Shui to practice. Feng Shui is about making you feel comfortable, supported, rejuvenated, and at peace.

A clear path in your home

As you begin your journey into the world of Feng Shui, you start to realize that your home and workspace reflect your inner condition. You see that these spaces are actually extensions of who you are and how you express yourself in the world. Every object, as well as your choice of color, lighting, and décor in your home or workspace reflects your life experiences and the choices you've made.

Feng Shui is about making you feel comfortable, supported, rejuvenated, and at peace.

Working with Feng Shui principles shifts the outer patterns of your environment, and thus supports inner change. It helps you gain insight into how to move forward in a way that serves you best. Take, for example, how wonderful you feel when you do a spring cleaning. You find old, misplaced items and clear the piled-up clutter. You gain new clarity— a clearer path in the home, so to speak. Also, your subconscious feels lighter because it no longer reacts to the overwhelming number of objects, and no longer registers, "I couldn't let a bit more stuff into my life—I'm full!" This is a small example of how your inner and outer conditions mirror each other. Feng Shui is a means of accessing a deeper understanding, and brings light to the patterns in each of us.

Subtle impressions of your environment

As we discussed, there are a number of factors that influence your perception of a space. On a physical level it's the color, the lighting, the kind of furniture and decorations. On a subtle level it is the energy of

Everything around you is alive and interacts with your energy.

All of the martial arts are based on the ability to use the body as a vessel to direct energy. Athletes are usually very aware of their body, and many find that the following types of exercises help them take advantage of their total body power.

items interacting and registering on your subconscious. Keep in mind that all colors and structures have a vibration. Everything around you is alive and interacts with your energy. Physics says that every object is molecular—its density, quality, and structure are in constant movement. Because your blood contains metal, you are constantly adjusting to the magnetic fields around you. These fields are influenced by the items in the space and their elemental qualities.

Responding to your environment

Imagine how you feel when you walk into a new place. Countless bits of information impress your perception, stimulating your senses as you respond to the new environment. Let's say you walk into a restaurant and have the feeling in the pit of your stomach that says, "I don't want to be here." Your eyes may have focused on the pea-green curtains, which you don't like; but if you take the time to get a clear impression, you will receive a deeper understanding of the room. By attuning yourself to the more subtle impressions, such as whether the space is too dark, not open enough, full of sadness or feels hectic, you tap into your own intuition, and are able to use Feng Shui from an energetic perspective.

Your body/mind system

Your body is an amazing computer that records everything that happens to you. How memories are stored remains a mystery. Melancholic memories can surface for no apparent reason. Joy can bubble up at any given time. As you become aware of how your surroundings trigger thoughts and emotions, you realize how complex you really are. For example, imagine yourself walking down a street. Out of the blue you feel sad and have no explanation why. Two blocks before, you had passed a cocker spaniel similar to the one that ran away when you were young. Although you saw the dog, you didn't consciously register the memory of your lost pet because you were thinking about the dinner menu for your party that evening. Nevertheless the emotion still surfaced when you saw the dog. By becoming aware of yourself, your mental patterns, and the effect that the environment has on you, you allow a shift in consciousness.

Reflecting on your world

Watching how you interact with the world can be an exciting process of self-discovery. One woman I know became enthralled watching her patterns emerge, and took a few minutes in the morning to center herself, which heightened her ability to observe herself throughout the day. In the evening she took the time to process what she noticed, and saw patterns dissolving just by bringing awareness to them. This worked well for her because while she was in a peaceful state, her subconscious, cellular, emotional, and mental memories had a chance to surface into her consciousness.

Grounding exercises

Grounding exercises are helpful in achieving a peaceful state. Doing these kinds of exercises promotes a grounded, centered feeling. They also strengthen your ability to reflect on how you interact with the world and help you connect with your intuition.

The Tree

Stand with your feet at shoulder length apart. Bend your knees slightly and let your hips relax. Place your attention on your feet and how they make contact with the floor. After you have connected with the floor, picture yourself as a tree with roots. See the roots moving from the bottom of your feet down past the floor, growing deep within the earth. Use a gentle breath to relax yourself. On every exhale, feel your roots growing deeper and deeper within the earth. You will start to feel your mind disengage. As you focus more and more on your feet and the ground, you may feel as if energy is moving upward from the earth.

Feeling the space around you

Once you have grounded yourself, you can extend your awareness to the space around you with the following exercise:

Close your eyes. Allow yourself to relax and let go. Once you feel a strong connection and are relaxed, focus your attention on feeling the space around you. This could be your home, office, or anywhere you

A quick note

Some people are naturally grounded and automatically feel their connection with the ground. They access this energy naturally and appear as if they are solidly on the ground. Then there are others, like myself, who respond to this exercise by thinking, "Oh, I have feet." To this day I have to remind myself not to just think about my feet but to really drop my full attention and feeling into my feet and to focus on my breath. If at first you experience difficulty connecting with the ground, stick with it. With a little practice this will feel very natural.

choose. Refrain from evaluating or judging your impressions. Notice where you feel these impressions in your body. Is it a mental, emotional, or physical response? If it is physical, go a bit further. Is it in your heart, or maybe a gut feeling?

An objective look at your creation

Looking objectively at your own home can be more difficult than walking into a new place because of your familiarity with it. To look objectively requires disengaging the mind and seeing what surfaces. With this in mind, walk through your home and note the spaces that you and your family members gravitate to. Some parts of the house seem natural for a bedroom, restful and recharging. Some areas are more useful for settling in with a good book, others are great for exercising.

Some parts of the house seem natural for a bedroom, restful and recharging.

See where your children feel best doing their homework. Notice where your bedroom is and how well you sleep at night. See how much sun enters into each room and at what time of day. Notice how you feel in each area of your home and ask yourself:

- What is the flow like from room to room?
- Is there a place in your home where you like to read and relax?
- Are there other places where you feel highly charged and able to focus on business and doing paperwork?

What you want to create in your space

Once you have looked at your home with a new set of eyes you can create what you want in your space and in your life. This boils down to defining what your intention is. Consider what kind of activities you perform in each room. What kind of feeling do you want each room to have? After you have clarified your intention, it will be easy to see what Feng Shui recommendations fit best and support you. The next few chapters offer a number of tools for evaluating your spaces and creating harmonious atmospheres in which to live and work.

Chapter 2

The *Five Elements* and Nine Star Ki Astrology

The Feng Shui practice uses tools to create an intentional space, just as a carpenter uses a hammer and saw to build a new building. Learning to use these tools is like learning to dance. You learn the moves, familiarize yourself with the steps, and practice. Then one day you find yourself dancing *without thinking*. You are in the flow of the dance, and the dance moves through you naturally. This is the idea behind Feng Shui. Let the tools inspire you and point you in the right direction, then let your own inner knowing lead the way.

The Five Elements

Some of the Feng Shui tools include the use of color, compass directions, land topography, and Nine Star Ki Astrology, all of which are based on the Five Elements. The ancient Taoist sages described the Five Elements of energy from their observations of the natural world. Nine Star Ki, Feng Shui, *I Ching*, and acupuncture are all based on these Five Elements: water, tree, fire, earth, and metal. Each element is not static, but linked to the next element, making a complete cycle.

We all have the five elements actively working inside us. To understand and actually apply Feng Shui and to use these principles, you need to have a clear understanding of the philosophy on which all of this is based.

The rhythms of life

The elements express archetypal energy, or how energy moves constantly and cyclically in the natural world. From the birth and death of galaxies far away, to the life span of a firefly, the cycle of life is evident. One way to view the cycle is the following:

Water	*the womb*
Tree	*the birthing process and toddlerhood*
Fire	*teenage to early adulthood*
Earth	*middle age*
Metal	*old age to death, and then returning to water*

Another way of looking at this is using the actual elements involved:

- Water supports and allows a tree or plant to grow.
- Trees provide the fuel for a fire to burn.
- Once a fire has burned, ashes fall to the ground, creating earth.
- The earth solidifies over time and creates ores or metals deep in the ground.
- As the metal condenses over time it again becomes liquid, leading us back to water.

The Five Elements
and the rhythms of life

Some of the Feng Shui tools include the use of color, compass directions, land topography, and Nine Star Ki Astrology, all of which are based on the Five Elements.

We call this cycle the supportive cycle, and it is represented in the diagram to the right by the arrows along the outside of the circle.

There is another cycle that I like to call the "moderator cycle," which is represented in the diagram by the arrows flowing on the inside.

When in balance:

- Water moderates fire, keeping it from raging out of control.
- Fire warms metal, allowing it to become more flexible.
- Metal moderates tree, making sure it does not rise up too fast.
- Tree moderates soil by keeping it from being too solid.
- Soil moderates water by giving it a form to adapt to, such as the bank of a river.

When out of balance:

- Water can extinguish fire.
- Fire can melt metal.
- Metal can cut or chop down tree.
- Tree can break up and separate earth.
- Earth can stagnate water.

Another metaphor for the elemental cycle is the times of day. The water element represents the hours between midnight and dawn, when all is still and quiet. The tree element takes over from the break of dawn until just before the heat of the day, and represents active, upward energy. During the midday hours the fire element blooms with full activity. When the sun begins to move toward sunset, from afternoon to early evening, the earth element begins to slow the cycle down. Then the metal element cycles into stillness from the evening to midnight, until the water element begins again.

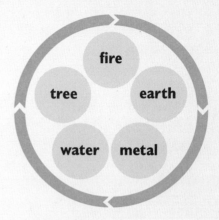

Supportive Cycle

Moderator Cycle

9

Water energy suggests being in the flow, feeling the rhythms that cycle through life.

The Water Element
Potential

Let's start with the water element. At the beginning and end of the cycle is the mysterious water element. The energy of water has a floating, adaptable quality, as well as tremendous power and endurance. For example, notice how the solid rocks at the ocean's edge are worn away by the repeated pounding of the surf. Water also holds the potential for life, like the womb where we are nurtured and prepare for birth.

The season associated with water is winter. Winter is a time when activity is beneath the surface. On the outside, it seems that not much is happening, but deep inside, the potential waits to blossom. The time of the day related to the water element is from midnight to the early hours of the morning. Again, a time of deep quiet, waiting for the light of day. In our personal life one can say the element of water governs study time and the potential to learn about ourselves and our path in life. It is the water element within us that gives us our willpower and our strength to endure. It is believed that the water element has a great deal to do with our genetics, or what we inherited from our ancestors.

Water energy suggests being in the flow, feeling the rhythms that cycle through life, as well as unconscious dreams and trusting oneself. It is related to following your path in life and doing what you love.

The Tree Element
Ideas

Tree energy suggests active participation, new ideas, and reaching out.

From water and our potential, we move into the tree element, which has a rapid, upward movement. It is the energy of birth or springtime and new beginnings. We feel this energy within us when we start any new project and have new ideas. We especially feel this element in the spring-time. Many of us feel the need literally to spring-clean, to allow the new life force to express through us. The water element was expressed as our time in the womb developing; the actual moment of birth and babyhood most exemplifies the rising energy of the tree element.

The time of day that relates to the tree energy is dawn, the birth of a new day. Have you ever awakened on a spring morning early with the sun shining brightly? You feel charged and full of life—you want to jump out of bed and conquer the world. This is the energy of the tree element, a get-up-and-go movement, which reaches up like the growth of plants, flowers, and trees. In our interactions this energy manifests as planning, initiative, and decision making.

Tree energy suggests active participation, new ideas, reaching out, and receiving input, as well as communing with nature and animals. It is also about being in touch with our bodies and what motivates us.

The Fire Element

Blossoming

From the springtime we move to summer and the fire element. Summer is a time of high energy and of blooming and fruition. The fruits are on the vines and the flowers are in full bloom. The energy associated with this element is very active and expanded.

Fire energy rises, similar to tree energy, yet moves in many different directions. If you have ever watched a log fire you will see this quality. Fire is a highly excitable energy that moves constantly. The time of the day associated with the fire element is midday, when the sun is at its highest in the sky. The fire element has a natural warmth and sociability to it. Think of how difficult it is to contain fire—and how it can spread like wildfire. It is the time when we see the "fruits" of our planning in the spring stage. From the point of view of our life cycle, the fire element relates to our blossoming, and our reaching adulthood with a clear objective view of who we are and what we wish to achieve.

Fire energy suggests higher purpose, sunlight, openheartedness, fun, laughter, and networking. It is related to the feeling of being connected with the grand picture of humanity and of being in this world for a reason.

Fire energy suggests higher purpose, sunlight, open-heartedness, fun, laughter, and networking.

Earth energy is about nurturing, receiving, balance, stability, feeling total support from the universe and our choices.

The Earth Element
Gathering

This leads us to the next element, earth or late summer. The high point of the summer has been reached and the energy settles down to gather. The direction of movement is downward and consolidating. After the fire has reached its peak it starts to lose its brightness, and ashes fall down and gather. Think of the nourishment we receive from mother earth—it supports all of life.

The time of day is afternoon, the energy of the sun is sinking. It is the time of day that encourages slowing down. The time of life relates to our maturity, our settling down into the truth of who we discovered ourselves to be at the fire stage.

Earth energy is about nurturing, receiving, balance, stability, and feeling total support from the universe and our choices. It is about loving oneself enough that the overflow embraces everyone close to us. It is about boundaries and support systems.

The Metal Element
Completion

As the sun starts to set and night begins to close in, the next element, metal, takes the stage. This is a strong, contracting force that began with the gathering of the earth, which then forms metals and ores. The energy of metal uses the consolidated energy from the earth element to create in the world. It is the opposite of springtime; it is autumn, the season of reaping.

Metal energy is about intuition, clarity, completion, and wisdom.

The time of the day is evening. The time of life is old age. Metal energy represents the evening of our life, a time for retiring and settling in for a cozy night. It's the stage in a project, for example, when everything comes together and is completed.

Metal energy is about intuition and clarity. It's about completion and wisdom, as well as trusting our decisions.

Each element leads to the next, bringing its own gifts to the whole. One creates the next. Without one the whole would not exist. Together they create balance.

The elements are associated with colors, directions, seasons, organs, and much more. The following chart lists the elements and their associations:

Element	Water	Tree	Fire	Earth	Metal
Color	Black Blue	Green	Red	Yellow	White Gray
Compass Direction	North	East	South	Center	West
Organ	Kidney Bladder	Gallbladder Liver	Heart Small Intestine	Stomach Spleen Pancreas	Large Intestine Lungs
Season	Winter	Spring	Summer	Beginning and End of Every Season	Fall
Celestial Influence	Mercury	Jupiter	Mars	Earth	Venus
Nine Star Ki Number	1	3 4	9	2 5 8	6 7

In sillier moments, I like to think of the elements as types of dogs, such as the following:

Tree   Jack Russell, boundless energy

Fire   Schnauzer, showy and attracts attention

Earth   Great Dane, grounded and solid

Metal   Springer Spaniel, focused with a bright mind

Water   Yellow Lab, relaxed and adaptable

Nine Star Ki: Feng Shui Astrology

Nine Star Ki and Feng Shui are truly holistic systems that encompass all of the human experience. These ancient methodologies are best explained with analogies that describe the energy of each element. Nine Star Ki Astrology comes from an ancient Chinese text called the *I Ching* (pronounced "e king"). The *I Ching,* or *Book of Changes,* is perhaps the oldest book that comes to us from the ancient Taoist philosophers. It says that all of life is based on the principle of change. In fact, it is often said that the only constant in life is change!

Changes occur in the natural world, cycling and repeating every year, month, day—down to minutes and seconds. The natural cycles are represented by eight trigrams of the *I Ching.* Each of the trigrams represents the quality and direction of energy. (The trigrams are outlined in Chapter 6.) The central trigram adds the ninth element, resulting in Nine Star Ki. These trigrams and the energies they represent are then related to personality types.

Your Nine Star Ki chart includes a combination of two or three elements.

You have different elemental energies, depending on your time of birth, season, and year. Nine Star Ki explains how your elemental nature manifests in your personality and in your interaction with others. (These qualities of energy are also represented by the compass directions, which are discussed in Chapter 6.)

Three numbers represent these energies in your Nine Star Ki chart. In this book we will look at the first two. Your first number represents your true essence, or essential nature (your constitutional nature). The second number represents your emotional nature. The third represents how you appear to others. Understanding the relationship between your essential nature and your emotional nature is my focus in this book.

The personality types

Each personality type in Nine Star Ki is broken down into energy types. The elements describe the types of personality. Water, for example, relates to flowing and mysteriousness. The fire personality is the opposite. Sparks fly—it's hot and the energy moves up and out. Each personality has a very different expression.

There are nine basic Nine Star Ki personalities. The metal and tree elements have been broken down into sub-energies, so they both have two possible categories: the three-tree and four-tree personalities, and the six-metal and seven-metal personalities. Earth has three sub-energies, including the two-earth, five-earth, and eight-earth personalities. Water and fire have only one possible number each, one-water and nine-fire.

Nine Personalities

Nine Star Ki sheds light on the different ways that we communicate.

Nine Personalities

- **one**   water
- **three** tree
- **four**   tree
- **nine**   fire
- **two**   earth
- **five**   earth
- **eight** earth
- **six**   metal
- **seven** metal

Your chart includes a combination of two or three elements. So, when you use the charts in the Nine Star Ki Appendix to figure out your Nine Star Ki chart, you might find, for example, that you are a two-earth for your first (constitutional) number/element and a nine-fire for your second (emotional) number/element. Your numbers are then (2,9).

You may relate more to one of your personality types than the other, or see a little of your nature in each description. It is the interaction of your constitutional and emotional natures that make you uniquely who you are. The descriptions in the Appendix are general, and are meant to describe the energetic gist of each Nine Star Ki personality and how it is expressed. Also included in the Appendix are famous people's Nine Star Ki charts. (It's fun to read about famous people who have the same chart as you!)

Relating to others: How Nine Star Ki can help you

Nine Star Ki also explains why we sometimes have differences and difficulties in relationships with others. It sheds light on the different ways that we communicate. If you have insight into how someone close to you, such as your teenager or spouse, perceives life, you are one step closer to understanding and supporting them on their journey.

By recognizing the nine personality types in this system, you will realize that each person expresses his or her elemental energy. You begin to see that some of the personality types fit together perfectly, naturally, and supportively; and that some combinations are harder, such as fire and water, because although each is equally valid, they combat each other. More effort is needed to put together someone who is like water (more underneath the depths of life) with someone who is like fire (demonstrative and extroverted). Interestingly enough, these two types are attracted to each other because each demonstrates qualities the other feels they do not have in themselves. Water gives fire depth and vision, while fire offers water warmth.

For example, some people are naturally bold, outward, and expressive. Others are inward, quiet, and contemplative. Some people are both of those at the same time. Nine Star Ki explains these qualities of how we express ourselves. It gives us permission to be who we are. Most often a person sees himself or herself as needing to change or separate from others. For example, my daughter is bold and her energy emanates into other people's spaces. For those who are less expressive and more inward, her energy can feel invasive.

Understanding that she expresses energy differently than I do allows me to have a broader perspective on how to be in relationship with her. Instead of wanting her to be more like me, I can realize it's not about how to change her but how to help her use her energy to serve her as a person. This extends further to say her natural, boundless energy serves the whole. Her energy also allows her to be warm and express her love fully. Her nature allows her to accomplish things that she sets out to do. These kinds of insights help you take a step back from your relationships and view them with new eyes, honoring each person for who they are.

Some people are naturally bold and expressive.

Element	Supports	Controls	Works together
			if in BALANCE, drains if not.
Water	Tree	Fire	Metal
Tree	Fire	Soil	Water
Fire	Soil	Metal	Tree
Soil	Metal	Water	Fire
Metal	Water	Tree	Soil

Nine Star Ki allows you deeper insight into your relationships with your loved ones, family, friends, and coworkers. It is a modality that supports each individual in a home or office, as well as the family or business unit as a whole. I have seen all kinds of groups gain profound insights when they are given an objective view of how they coexist energetically and emotionally.

Making the most of your business relationships

Many professionals use the insight gained through Nine Star Ki to aid them in relationships, management, and life choices. By applying Feng Shui concepts and addressing the strengths and weaknesses of the individuals within the group, you can capitalize on this knowledge and achieve optimum "flow." For example, situating each employee in the most appropriate place within the building allows him or her to blossom, perform to his or her fullest, and increase positive results in your business.

Nine Star Ki assists individuals in seeing themselves with a new set of eyes. Seeing their innate gifts allows people to accept themselves and others unconditionally, without having to be like anyone else. No one can do everything, so why not work together and utilize what each person brings to the whole?

Nine Star Ki allows you deeper insight into your relationships with your loved ones, family, friends, and co-workers.

No one can do everything; so why not work together and utilize what each person brings to the whole?

Supportive relationships

Once you have figured out your Nine Star Ki numbers, you can see how people fit in your life. There is a balance to the five elements and the personality types. Each naturally moves to the next, yet it would move out of control if not balanced by its opposing forces. In the chart on the previous page you see that water supports the growth of tree, helps fire to calm down or to be put out, and helps the metal move to the next element. There is an interchange between the metal and water. You can also see that a metal person supports a water person and helps bring clarity. A water person helps a metal person see the big picture and slow down to relax. Yet water can also drain the metal if it is overpowering.

Finding out more about yourself

You can learn more about your Nine Star Ki Astrology by looking up your date of birth in the Nine Star Ki Appendix. Listed there also are full details of how to calculate your Nine Star Ki Astrology chart. In the Appendix you will also find descriptions of each of the personality types, including how they relate to the elements and each other.

Chapter 3

Color *your world*

Color has a profound effect on your well-being.
I've seen color transform people's lives.
It can make all the difference in how you feel in your
home or business. You can use color to create a
special feeling, whether you are looking to recharge,
relax, enliven, or stimulate. See which colors feel
best to you. Then when you think of decorating your
living and work spaces, choose to surround yourself
with color schemes that amplify your intention.
If your intention is to increase the creative energy
in your workplace, orange and red accents can spark
your creative fire and enliven your environment.

Creating a cozy community

When there is more than one person in a house, the goal is to harmonize and create a community environment that will support each member of the home. You may choose colors for a main floor that are warm and inviting, such as shades of yellow, light mauve, putty, or warm salmon. These colors bring people out of their heads (or mental focus) and into their feeling centers. Many other colors work perfectly; see how each color makes you feel.

One woman I know preferred a shade of putty because it helped her ground her energy, while the warmer colors made her feel too hectic. So pay attention to how your mind, body, and energy level feel around certain colors. Many people are surprised how great they feel around colors they would not normally like. Take notice of the colors in places you go. Restaurants and shops often have shades of gold and warm colors that you wouldn't have thought of using if you hadn't realized how terrific you felt in that space. Bolder colors, as well as wallpaper patterns, can also be fun and uplifting.

Many people are surprised how great they feel around colors they would not normally like.

Transforming learning environments

The following story illustrates how color made a remarkable difference in students' ability to feel comfortable and more in tune with their creativity and their ability to work together.

Recently I was called by the administrators of a school that was having problems with enrollment. They felt that something was missing from the learning environment. One big issue, they had found, was that the cinder-block gray color that dominated the school walls felt depressing and dark. After I met with the staff they decided to do an experiment with color and its effects on the children's well-being. Each class was given a chance to vote on several colors best suited to the location of their particular classroom.

One eighth grade class created a one-wall "wall art" project where they could paint a scene from one of the places in the world that they had studied. The base color they chose was a soft yellow. One child said it made the room feel alive and uplifted. Before it was painted, she said, she had always felt that her classroom was stuck in the basement and that it felt cold. That same classroom is now where everyone gathers to discuss ideas and work together on projects. It is now a much friendlier environment.

Another classroom was painted green with a sponge-paint color over it; the teacher remarked how inspired the children were to take on new projects. One child said that the classroom gave her the feeling that she was in nature, and she loved all the changes, including the paint color.

The math teacher saw a major shift in her classroom's behavior. She had three difficult children who seemed to get the whole class going. Her classroom was painted a terra-cotta color, which added warmth and grounding. One child who had been diagnosed as having attention deficit disorder reported she was so happy to be in the classroom, whereas before it was painted she could not wait to go outside. How often are we in a hotel or office space that we long to remove ourselves from and go home? We can all relate to the student's feeling of wanting to get outside quickly.

The science teacher told me that enrollment had increased since they revamped the school. More important, though, was that the children had a very positive response to the color changes. She noticed they were less restless, more grounded and more receptive. She herself felt uplifted and less bogged down by her workload; she now had much more energy.

Remarkable changes happen when you add warm, nurturing colors to a learning environment. Every setting is unique, but I recommend taking a large piece of paper and painting it a color you are considering for a room. Then put it up and see how the color feels in the room throughout the day. You will be surprised to see that the color will change from morning to evening. You may need to add more depth or perhaps tone it down. You may also need to try variations on the colors you like to find the one that best suits your needs.

Remarkable changes happen when you add warm, nurturing colors to a learning environment.

Do note that paints can be very toxic. There are brands that put out healthy alternatives. Sherwood Williams makes Healthspek, and another is Glidden 2000, which are much easier on the lungs and the nervous system. My advice is, after painting a building air it out for two weeks or more before occupying it. Fumes can make it difficult for people to focus and concentrate, not to mention feel healthy. Schools need to realize that even with the windows open, breathing fumes for eight hours is not good for anyone, especially children.

Catching attention

Color can be used for myriad purposes, in addition to creating community. Take, for example, McDonald's, where yellow is used with bright red to draw people in and get attention. This does not mean you necessarily would frequent the restaurant, but you certainly know it's there. Yellow psychologically has the power to gather and bring people together. For many businesses I have recommended yellow in combination with other colors to enliven the setting.

The media and the world of advertising use color as a selling tool.

The media and the world of advertising use color as a selling tool. They use reds to fire you up, blues to soothe and calm you down, and color combinations to get your attention in all types of ways. Two colors together can sometimes fall short of catching a customer's eye, but adding a third color can create the dynamics needed to attract people's attention. The right combination of colors can be a profound tool for achieving your goal.

The colors and the elements

Whether the business world is aware of it or not, they play with the elemental qualities of color. In Feng Shui, the Five Elements are used as a framework to explore colors and their qualities. Depending on the shades and how they make you feel, colors can fall into different element categories. For example, salmon has not only fire energy in it, but also the earth element.

Element	Water	Tree	Fire	Fire/Earth	Earth	Metal
Colors	Shades of	Shades of	Shades of	Shades of	Shades of	Shades of
	blue black turquoise deep purples	green	orange-yellow yellow red bright yellows red-pinks	salmon peach pink	brown tan beige off-white with warmth	white gray silver metallics
Qualities	fluidity	movement new ideas	expansive charging	warm nurturing	grounding nurturing	clarifying, defining

The chart above describes the colors and their elemental qualities. Its purpose is to spark ideas and give you ways to create movement. It isn't meant to limit you in any way. Use it as a reference, but first trust your intuition. For example, you may want only gray and white on your walls because they are familiar to you. Then you decide to venture into the world of color because you went to a restaurant that had colors on the wall that made you feel great. Then you read this chart and it said that one of those colors, say green, supports you. The point is, the chart is here to open up possibilities, not to limit you. It doesn't imply, Don't use a particular color. The message is, Play with color and see what it can do for you.

You may find that you are a seven-metal but you love green. Look to see what shade you are attracted to. Maybe it makes you feel recharged and that is what you need right now. Go for it—don't underestimate the power of color!

> **Water colors** support three- and four-tree people, and are calming for six- and seven-metal people. In some cases, they may calm the fire personality.

Play with color and see what it can do for you. Go for it— don't underestimate the power of color!

Tree colors support nine-fire people, and help one-water people move forward. In some cases, they may inspire the earth personality.

Fire colors support two-, five-, and eight-earth people, and help redirect tree people. In some cases, they may warm the metal personality.

Earth colors support six- and seven-metal people, and calm nine-fire people. In some cases, they may refocus the water personality.

Metal colors help support one-water people, and create movement for two-, five-, and eight-earth people. In some cases, they may redirect the tree personality.

Warming up your life

Color absorbs light and warmth. White reflects light back out.

The following story is a great example of how the use of Nine Star Ki helped determine supportive colors for my client, an interior designer. She was very interested in using Feng Shui principles to help her clients, and she felt that starting in her own home was the best way to learn.

When I went to her home, I found it well designed, with sufficient energy circulation. During the consultation, she shared personal details with me in hopes that I might have some insight for her. Her parents had died recently and she had just split up with her partner. She had inherited her parents' house and painted the interior white with a blue hint to it. Her life felt at a standstill, and she felt unable to move forward. She wanted to add spice to her life and attract new friends and clients. Consulting the Nine Star Ki Astrology, I found she had two earth numbers in her chart, which told me she was an information warehouse and that moving forward could be hard for her.

My main recommendation to her was to bring warm colors into the house. The white walls had accentuated her mental activity and the blue hint was depressing. She needed a combination of warmth with an uplifting feeling in her sanctuary. Colors such as salmon with a touch of fire energy would also support her, as well as ground and warm up her home. She chose a light, Southwestern peach color for her walls and a lighter version of the same color for the trim. The lighter trim color opened up the windows. (A darker trim tends to close in and define a window—she needed the opposite.) The beautiful tile floor had gone unnoticed until she added the warm color on the walls—then the floor came alive.

She had curtains that were heavy and covered a quarter of the window. I suggested she take them down to open up the light capacity. She added pleated, colored window shades that were completely invisible when up. She chose the kind that cover only the lower half for privacy and leave the upper part open. Beautiful sunlight, which represents fire energy and supports her earth nature, now enters her home. The warm color on the walls absorbs the sunlight, whereas the white had reflected light back out.

Her house became a place she loved to come home to, and now she even loves to entertain. On a psychological note, the small change in color alone brought her to a new level of vitality, which funneled into all aspects of her life. She made other adjustments that helped support her goals, and she reports that her outlook is positive and her energy level has skyrocketed. She feels like she is really living instead of just existing.

The shades of color

The following section lists a more complete description of the colors and their elemental qualities. As you read, try imaging the colors or find examples and sense how they feel. Each color shade is different, and it is well worth taking the time to find your supportive colors. I have seen people who have light deprivation tendencies (people who live in areas that do not get very much sunlight, particularly in winter) combat depression with colors that recharge them. I have seen hospitals transform into healing environments with color as their main tool. (In the "Healthcare" chapter there are stories that describe the profound healing power of color.)

Each color shade is different, and it is well worth taking the time to find your supportive colors.

Color **Yellow**   Element **Earth**

Soft yellows such as honey or glowing sunlight have a warming effect, and are comforting and nurturing. Yellow supports the solar plexus, allowing people to be at ease and feel supported. Yellow is a gathering color; it can be used in places that need to promote sociability and security. Yellow flowers exude sunshine and happiness. Because yellow has a settling effect, it supports digestion and the nervous system.

Bright yellow is very electric and energizing. A woman I recently met at a talk I gave had just painted her bedroom bright yellow and thought her insomnia was related to the color of the walls. Many other factors influenced her, but bright yellow bedroom walls can be overly stimulating and not conducive to a settled night's sleep.

Gemstones that support the solar plexus and nourish digestion: citrine, gold topaz, moonstone, dolomite, yellow jade, mother-of-pearl, apatite

Color **Red**   Element **Fire**

Red attracts attention. It can stimulate passion, yet if not balanced, it can raise anger. Red can activate and enliven a room. Fresh red flowers are bright and can open the heart. Combined with other colors, red can be a power color in business settings. Tiles with a red tinge can be perfect to brighten a kitchen and add a warm, inspiring feel.

I did a consultation for an interior designer in Florida whose house was decorated with black and white checks and red accents. The red made a bold statement because of the contrasting colors she used. Her flare to combine these colors showed an enormous amount of expression and boldness. The quote from *Star Trek,* "Boldly going where no one has gone before," is her business motto. She expresses who she is in her surroundings so beautifully.

Color **Orange**   Element **Fire**

Orange sparks creative energies. It is related to the second chakra, where creative, sexual, and emotional energies reside. Shades of orange can be great colors to have in an office to stimulate activity and getting out in the world.

Yellow

Yellow clothing is uplifting and offers warmth and cheeriness.

Red

Bright red clothing attracts attention, expresses strength and boldness. If you are prone to anxiety and overheating, red may not be the color for you; cooler colors can help create BALANCE.

If you work in a red or orange room, take notice of how you feel in that space. Many of my clients feel that red helps bring up their energy level when they are working with deadlines.

Red and orange-red are not recommended for bedrooms unless passion is your goal. Along with passion will come anger and a short temper, so I recommend subtle shades bordering the pinks if you want red tones in your bedroom.

Gemstones that promote rejuvenation and energizing: coral, garnet, fire opal, ruby, carnelian, orange calcite, peach adventurine, cinnabar

Color **Blue**   Element **Water**

Blue is usually a cool color and has a relaxing, liquefying effect. Blue has the ability to bring one deep inside, as it is an introspective color. Used in healing rooms and meditation spaces, it promotes vision and movement into the unknown. On a subconscious level blue has a balancing effect, so it's a good color to wear when upset, nervous, or hyperactive.

Professional institutions often use blue to communicate a sense of official business. Police officers, airline personnel, and institutions that want to convey a sense of presence and continuity wear blue. Businessmen and women choose blue to signal confidence and efficiency to the world.

However, too much blue can literally make you blue. It can be depressing and stagnating if it is the predominant color in a home. Blue may be your favorite color, but because of the gray tones often in blue, it's best used as an accent color to offset other colors with elegance.

Gemstones that support the emotions and relaxation: sapphire, blue topaz, blue aventurine, angelite, apophyllite, aquamarine, blue calcite, celestite, chrysoprase, blue opal, sodalite

Color **Green**   Element **Tree**

Green can be healing and recharging. It symbolizes renewal and the season of spring. Green walls in a home bring nature into the living environment. Plants bring a touch of nature into a home or office; they are vibrant and symbolize growth. Green is a regal color, and is often

Orange

Red-orange clothing inspires creativity and is energizing.

Blue

Wear blue clothing to feel calm, restful, fluid, and to stimulate new options and visions.

Green

Bright and deep greens are for stimulation, and ocean greens for relaxation and health.

White

White clothing can be official and mentally stimulating. White can also represent purity and beauty, in the case of flowers and wedding arrangements. Sterile environments are usually overly white to the point of being cold and unfriendly.

used in museums and royal buildings. (Gold often accompanies green.) Softer tones of green are great for an office space, making the occupant feel enlivened and motivated to accomplish the task at hand. Green also is a great color for athletic centers.

Green tile floors bring a light, springtime feel to a room. One woman inventor, who had all green bathroom fixtures, loved soaking in her green, sea-colored tub. She said that every time she took a bath she was filled with new ideas. The water and tree elements supported her income because the bathroom was where she got her inspiration.

Gemstones that help promote playfulness, heartfelt feelings, and health: peridot, calcite, dioptase, fluorite, emerald, jade, green tourmaline, chrysocolla, chrysoprase, malachite

Color **White** Element **Metal**

White is a versatile color and is used as a base in many settings. It is mentally stimulating and tends to be stark. If you are not careful with it, it creates a home that feels like place to just hang your hat. What is a home? It is a place to recharge from a long day—it is your sanctuary. The trend today is to use too much white, which is not conducive to relaxing and recharging. A person who lives in a home with all white walls will tend to create a life where mental activity dominates. Contrary to most belief systems, outside light reflects back out when it hits a white wall. It can be cold and reflective. Color absorbs the natural light, bringing warmth to a room. White with other colors can brighten a room and be the canvas to show off colorful pieces.

Gemstones that support clarity and honesty: howlite, ivory, pearl, clear topaz, diamond, quartz

Color **Purple** Element **Combination, depending on hue**

Purples can be fun and whimsical. They also can be used to bring a regal feeling to a room. Purple can promote spiritual awareness. Purple can be a fun color to paint rooms where the focus is to relax and go with the flow. Combined with other colors, purple can take on many different effects. This is because purple can be a cool or warm color.

Gemstones that promote balanced spiritual awareness: amethyst, sugilite, tanzanite, violet tourmaline, charoite, ametrine, iolite

Color **Pink**   *Element* **Fire or earth, depending on hue**

Pinks have an earthy feel with a tinge of fire. They support intimacy and gathering, and can enliven a space. For a more masculine feel, mauves work in a similar fashion—combining earth and fire energies. Some pinks are gathering and others are activating.

Gemstones that promote heart support and love: rose quartz, rhodochrosite, strawberry quartz, pink tourmaline, turquoise, pink chalcedony, aphrodite

Color **Black**   *Element* **Water**

Black is a defining color. It is good to use as an accent in rooms—such as with furniture, iron tables, pots, and coatracks. Black can take on a very grounding, solid feel in furniture. In clothing and fabrics it tends to have a fluid, watery deep feel. Black can be elegant in combination with other colors such as gold and brown. Many people use blacks to define other colors in wood textures, fabrics, kitchen and bathroom fixtures. Iron is often black and is seen in outdoor railings, driveways, and mailboxes, which give a feeling of grounding to a building.

Black clothing can either attract or reflect energy. It offers protection and can feel businesslike.

Gemstones that support grounding, protection, and help promote peacefulness: hematite, black jade, jet, obsidian, onyx

Color **Brown**   *Element* **Earth**

Brown is a grounding color. Too much brown can be stagnating, and an overabundance of dark wood can be overwhelming. Leather furniture can be cozy and comforting. Furniture with brown accents can be elegant and earthy. Wood floors are a lovely surface, and the grain transitions can enhance a room as long as wood isn't the predominant element.

Gemstones that are grounding and offer a feeling of safety: leopard-skin jasper, amber

Purple

Wear purple to express a regal quality or to spark a wide perspective.

Pink

Pink clothing communicates a perky and comforting feeling.

Black

Black clothing can either attract or reflect energy. It offers protection and can feel businesslike.

Color **Silver**   *Element* **Metal**

Silver strengthens mental clarity and can be used in lighting fixtures and areas that need focus and definition.

Gemstones that promote vision: marcasite, mica, tigereye, tiger iron

Color **Gold**   *Element* **Metal**

Gold is uplifting, attracting, and a beautiful accent color. This color can be stabilizing and balancing. Gold frame pictures and mirrors can add elegance and definition. Gold metal fixtures can be reflective and can be used where the metal element is needed.

Gemstones that promote learning, clarity, and positive feelings: gold, pyrite, copper

your cherished **Belongings**

Each belonging in your sanctuary holds not only emotional connections but also energetic dynamics, all of which affect your mental, emotional, and physical well-being. Keep in mind that all colors and structures have a vibration. Everything around you is alive and interacts with your energy. Physics says that every object is molecular—its density, quality, and structure are in constant movement. Because our blood contains metal, we are constantly adjusting to the magnetic fields around us. These fields are influenced by the items in the space and their elemental qualities.

Take a walk through your home. Look at each room and its contents from an energetic perspective. Allow the emotional connections to surface; for example, does the picture of your college roommate make your heart sing? How do the objects and colors in your home *really* affect you? Let go of your preconceived notions about your "favorite" knickknack and *feel* it. You might try the "Feeling the Space Around You" exercise in Chapter 1, directing your focus on an item in your home.

You may find that things you once loved no longer have the same meaning for you. Everyone grows and changes, and our environments need to reflect that new growth. Allow yourself to see and feel what really serves you *now*. It does not serve you to keep items that bring up bad memories or that do not nurture you in some way. Even if you feel lukewarm about something, consider replacing it with something you adore, something that makes you smile from head to toe. You deserve no less!

When you remove old items, replace their old vibration with a new feeling.

Symbols of the past

Gifts and old items are often strong reminders of past relationships and can hold energy from the relationship, as well as be strong subconscious reminders of the person who gave them to you. At a lecture I once gave about this topic, a girl in the audience shook her head, struck by a realization. Afterward she came up to me and told me she had an old boyfriend's bureau in her closet and had never connected it with the nauseous feeling she felt every time she opened the closet door. It turned out the boyfriend had treated her very badly, and her subconscious connected the bureau with the emotional state she had felt while being with him. Getting rid of the bureau freed her to move beyond her bad memories.

Another woman had kept all of her ex-husband's old belongings, which brought nothing but bad memories for her. She kept them because they were valuable and she felt she had control over his past actions. She ended up removing all of his things from the room, and reported that afterward she felt she had regained her soul—a freedom she hadn't experienced since she was a teen.

Even though the room was physically cleared, it still held an old, dark impression. She saged the room (burning sage is a tradition used in many cultures for purification) and sprayed orange cleaner. She had also asked monks to come and pray, but somehow the room didn't feel quite right. Then she called me to ask me how to clear the energy from the room. I recommended she replace the old vibration with a new vibration.

Intuitively she felt she had done wonderful things to clear the room, but agreed she needed to bring in a new vibration. I asked her how she wanted the room to transform. What would the room become? She decided to have a party with children, laughter, cards, music, and singing because she intended that the room be a creative, joyful space. She had her daughters return from college and invited women friends and their kids over to add vibrancy by eating, playing, and singing. It was a marvelous cure. Opening the windows to allow air to flow through made a big difference. Adding new curtains, furniture, and uplifting pictures helped as well. Now the third floor of her house feels like an added benefit instead of a gloomy museum.

A second look at secondhand

Your belongings not only trigger emotional memories, but also hold the vibration of previous owners. Think of "vibration" as a pattern such as the one made by a river running over a rock, year after year. Eventually the rock wears a pattern etched by the rushing waters. When a drought comes or the rock is taken out of the river, it is still marked by the currents even though it is no longer in the river. The same principle holds true for possessions—in time they take on their owner's patterns, like a pair of worn-in jeans.

I've heard thousands of stories of people taking on furniture because they felt obligated or felt they needed to get an affordable item even if they didn't like it. A classic example of this happened to a couple who had inherited an aunt's bed, which they used because they felt obligated to accept the inheritance. The bed was very old and felt heavy, as if it were laden with emotion. My sense was the bed did not support them or their romantic relationship. In fact, the bed felt cold, oppressive, and

Many cultures use vibrational tools such as a tuning fork, Tibetan temple bells, drums, and other gonglike items to clear a space.

prudish. The wife told me she didn't like the bed because it wasn't comfortable and she felt their relationship had been more romantic and passionate before they were given the bed.

They found out that the uncle had died in it and the widowed aunt had spent her remaining nights alone and very unhappy. Once they made the connections, they happily let go of it and bought a new bed, which they both loved.

Antiques, used furniture, and old curtains hold vibrations. Check to see how old items feel to you before you bring them into your sanctuary. Remember, it is *your* sanctuary; be careful not to put yourself under obligation to adopt items that do not serve you. Always choose things you love to bring into your home.

Balance your practical side with your heart

Don't let your practical nature always get the upper hand—give your heart and intuition a chance to guide you.

It's easy to get caught up in internal dialogue about what we should do or not do. We have multiple opinions and feelings about our possessions. Sometimes we hold on to items because we feel nostalgic or confused about what is "appropriate." By carefully examining what you keep around, you can begin to unwind the emotional ties and see clearly what really supports you. Don't let your practical nature always get the upper hand—give your heart and intuition a chance to guide you. You'll be surprised at what you discover!

An example of this was when a client of mine, who had been married to an antiques dealer, called me asking advice about selling her house, which was full of millions of dollars' worth of antiques. Although she had remarried, she hadn't changed her house. The dark antiques made the house feel tight, and constricted the flow in the home. Her new husband subconsciously felt the ex-husband's influence very strongly in the house but couldn't quite put his finger on it. On some level the antiques represented her past and weren't part of her new life with him.

She had two different feelings about the antiques. On one hand, her practical side knew they were worth a lot, but they didn't make her happy. She finally moved through her resistance and decided to contact an auctioneer. When the quote came back, she was shocked to find it higher than her own estimate!

By auctioning the majority of the pieces, yet keeping the pieces she truly wanted, she opened up the house, allowing more space and light in. After clearing out the things she didn't really love, her initial intention of selling the house slipped away. The new arrangement allowed her and her new husband to live in the present, in a house they both loved. She also felt new, transformational avenues open up to her that allowed her to feel lighter and able to let go of old patterns.

Liven up old mementos

One woman had an old iron coatrack with arms that stood out in her hallway. A little mirror in the middle allowed you to check your lipstick as you were going out the door. When I visited her, I shared a story about how old things can remind us of the past, and the woman started laughing, saying she had just remembered something profound. The coatrack was her grandmother's that she inherited when she bought her new house. She painted it and purified it with sage, then put it in the hall. As we talked she remembered how her grandmother would be extremely bossy and pull her and her siblings around the house by their ears. Now, every time she came home she would subconsciously be reminded of being bossed around.

Her memory helped her transform this old feeling. Instead of getting rid of the "old battle-ax" as she described it, she decided to paint the rack with fun, wild colors. She added silly pictures of animals and things she loved. A plant in the stand at the bottom gave it new life. Her sister came over and together they put silly glasses and hats on it. They took the cracked mirror out of the middle and added funny pictures of her brothers and sisters together. This was her new rack to come home to, reminding her of her grandmother's good points. Her entryway was now filled with laughter at the whimsical coatrack. It was now an empowering, lively, and fun piece of furniture.

Every object in a space holds a vibration and a certain memory or energetic input. Decide what supports you and makes you feel good. Give special attention to file cabinets and other places you store things. What is in those containers?

Fans

There are beautiful mood-enhancing fans that are functional too.
I've seen some that appear to be made of paper and look like a leaf that
would be fanned in front of Cleopatra. Some are called paddle fans
and they move through the air calmly, while beautifying any room. They
change the energetics of a space. (One manufacturer of this kind of
fan can be found on the web at Fanimation.com.)

Clutter

Many of my clients are aware of where they store their clutter and ask me
if they should clear up the piles before I arrive. Most of the time it is
useful to see where the clutter ends up, where the mail is left on entering
the home, where the kids drop their bags as they come in from school,
where things gravitate to in the house. It is definitely a topic that needs
defining. I will tell you a few stories that will make you laugh and you
can go from there.

The clutter had an overpowering effect on her psychological outlook.

Comforting clutter: Three refrigerators

A woman called me from New York while I was living in Florida. She
wanted to schedule an appointment for the next time I would be in New
York. She had already had three other Feng Shui consultants to her
apartment to give her recommendations. On arrival I knocked on her
door, and after about five minutes I heard her yell, "I'll be out in a
minute to let you in." A few minutes later she came out of a door down
the hall. She grabbed the doorknob in front of me and threw her hip
into the door. As it opened she said, "The door hasn't worked for years."
The door opened approximately twelve inches. She said, "Here, turn
sideways and you'll be able to get in." Behind the door was a floor-to-
ceiling stack of boxes. I figured she must have just moved in.

She had cleared a small path to the kitchen where she wanted me to
follow her. Boxes and other belongings lined the pathway. Upon entering
the eight-foot-by-six-foot kitchen we were greeted by two men who were
working there. She told me she had called me because she wanted to know
how to arrange her kitchen. The men were there to help her do this, as

well as build her a new set of cabinets. She said that from what she had read, appliance placement is crucial in Feng Shui and she needed to position her three refrigerators.

She was fond of the two older fridges because they had been in her family and they didn't make them like that anymore—definitely keepers. The new fridge was bought to hold freezer items as well, and the color was snazzy. After we discussed the fridge scenario and she was clear she needed all three fridges, we moved to the living room, where she moved a few boxes so we could sit down.

She proceeded to tell me that she had moved in ten years before and she was unsure if she wanted to stay there. So that I could get a view of the city, she pushed her moving clothes racks out of the way. She had four racks of clothing there, each one holding a different size. She explained that her weight fluctuated, and although she was a size four now, who could tell when she could be a size fourteen again? She told us that she was planning to donate a box or two of her late husband's medical books, but as for the other seventy-five boxes, she wanted advice on where they should go. She didn't feel she was sleeping well because her bedroom wall abutted her neighbor's bedroom. They were very loud at night and she wanted to block out the noise. She was tired of sleeping in the living room.

She stated outright that she did not want to discuss her living room, she had heard enough about that already. The clutter on some level reminded her of her husband and she was not ready to sort through it. After asking a few questions I realized that she felt friendless and as if no one was keeping in touch with her. She said she felt disconnected from the present and stuck in the past memories of her former life. She was frustrated that the seven needlepoint projects she had begun were sitting unfinished, and she was overwhelmed that nothing new seemed to enter into her life.

I explained to her that the overwhelming feeling directly correlated with her inability to find her way around her apartment. The clutter had an overpowering effect on her psychological outlook. All the boxes that hadn't been opened in years had to be sorted through so she could let go of the past. Finding the things in the boxes that she wanted to use

Find a new home for things you don't absolutely love.

would help her to feel like she was moving on in her life. Her goal was find what was useful and discard the rest. I suggested she find a new home for all the things that she didn't absolutely love.

Collectibles

Magazines, newspapers, and collectibles are often important to people. A neighbor of mine when I was growing up shared with me that after her mom died she had to go through piles and piles of full collections of old *Life* magazines and other subscriptions. The *National Geographic* collection took up half of her den, and the dust was a bit overwhelming. The question here is, What does such a collection do for you? Is it the memories? If it is a bear collection, do the cute little faces make you feel good? Recognize what the particular item does for you. If you have mixed feelings, try to evaluate what the pluses are. The main point is to have what you love in your space and try to clear out the excess, or find a space for each object where you can find it. If you end up as the storehouse for your relatives', children's, or friends' things, evaluate whether that serves your overall well-being.

If you end up as the storehouse for your relatives', children's, or friends' things, evaluate whether that serves your overall well-being.

Many of my clients have their children's wedding gowns, furniture, clothing or other things stored at their homes. Most often children in college do need a place for their belongings, but it doesn't hurt for them to sort through the piles and boxes. Most people do not want their dwelling place to be a storehouse, and I encourage them to ask the "storers" to come take their things. The driving theme behind why people don't ask others to come get their belongings is that they feel that they have the bigger space to keep them. Bottom line: It doesn't serve anyone to have boxes that don't belong to you in your sanctuary.

Clearing out, moving on

One woman had a room filled to the brim with old projects, miscellaneous items, paints, and old furniture. Her goal was to clear it out. The day I arrived she had already started getting rid of things and had begun to organize. After I left she cleared out the whole room. It took her hours. She filled a whole dumpster, and organized the rest. She felt great.

The next day she went to work and was fired. She called me in tears and said she'd been fired and could Feng Shui have caused that to happen?

When I was at her home we had discussed what was going well for her and what would she change in life if she could. Her biggest stress was her job. She felt that she never got credit for her efforts and she worked in a cramped space with poor lighting. My first question to her after she was fired was, "How do you feel about this?" I told her that clearing out the space might have made her feel terrific, yet it wouldn't have caused her to get fired. It would also certainly support new opportunities that might come into her life.

The more we talked, the more she expressed that it was mainly the unknown that frightened her. Her employers had actually offered her a job in a new department, in the field she had wanted to be in at the very start of her employment there. Furthermore, she stated they were moving her because her supervisor did not like her. They felt the move, if she chose to make it, would be best for all concerned. After she had stated all her fears, she decided to give the new job a try. She said she would call me after her first day at her new position. "Unbelievable!" was the first word out of her mouth when she called me. She had brought into her life a great boss, windows to look out of, a position where she could put her skills to use, and most of all, an actual joy about going to work. Understandably she had been used to the familiar, awful job, and the unknown, new job had frightened her. The overall experience led her to feel more supported in being herself in the world.

The Five Elements and their qualities in objects

Having taken a look at the belongings in your house and what they represent to you, you may want to bring in new vibrations. In doing so, it is helpful to look at them from the perspective of the Five Elements. The list below describes the elemental nature of objects. Use it as a guide to explore the energetic quality of items in your space or to bring in new influences to your home.

Look at the belongings in your house and see what they represent to you.

See which areas of your home are energized and which areas are calm.

Clay and Tile

Earth Element
Grounds; or if too much, can stagnate. Supports the metal element, pulls off fire element.

Glass and Mirrors

Water Element
Expands vision; or if too much, causes loss of clear boundaries. Supports the tree element, pulls off metal element.

Wood

Tree Element
Promotes upward, activating movement; or if too much, provokes irritability and is too activating. Supports fire element, pulls off water element.

Paper

Tree Element
Promotes upward, activating movement; or if too much, provokes irritability and is too activating. Supports fire element, pulls off water element.

Plaster

Earth Element
Grounds; or if too much, can stagnate. Supports the metal element, pulls off fire element.

Wicker and Bamboo

Tree Element
Promotes upward, activating movement; if too much, causes irritability and is too activating. Supports fire element, pulls off water element.

Silk, Cotton, Natural Fibers

Earth Element
Grounds; or if too much, can stagnate. Supports the metal element, pulls off fire element.

China

Earth Element
Grounds; or if too much, can stagnate. Supports the metal element, pulls off fire element.

Metal Objects	Metal Element
(Copper, Gold, Silver, Iron)	*Helps create clarity, definition, and*
Granite, Marble	*completion; can be cold. Supports the*
	water element, pulls off earth element.
Candles	Fire Element
	Activates, warms, illuminates. Supports the
	earth element, pulls off tree element.

Notice which elements are represented in the items in your home. See which areas of your home are energized and which areas are calm. See if you can glean any insights from the list above.

Balancing the elements

One woman I worked with was finding it difficult to move on after a divorce. After five years she decided she was wasting her time lamenting and wanted some advice. In her home she had an overabundance of heavy stone and clay statues that her husband had left with her. She also had tile floors in every room as well as a clay-plaster bedroom set, unusual as it may seem. The overabundance of the earth element supported her holding on instead of letting go. In essence it had stagnated her ability to go forward. Because she was not attached to most of the items, she sold them and acquired things that supported moving on.

Another woman's ex-husband had moved out after their divorce, but had left old framed family pictures in the home, as well as other belongings. She felt as if his old family relatives were living down in her basement. After a while she asked him to come remove them. When he came to get his things, she realized that the pictures were all framed in old dark wood frames and all of his belongings were fairly dark and heavy. After all the items were gone she felt as if the house was lighter and a new sense of movement flowed through the home.

Elements that support you

Sometimes this works the other way. One man had all wicker furniture and a log cabin-style home. He was a three-tree/four-tree personality so it made sense that he might be drawn to furnishings with the tree element in them. His main complaint was that he always started things, yet never

When he worked with the idea of BALANCE, *he found he became very centered and much more relaxed.*

got anything done. He asked what he could do to support his ability to finish projects and to feel less frazzled.

I suggested he introduce more grounding, warmer furnishings to his home. For example, the fire element draws off the excessive tree element, and the earth and metal elements would ground him and help him complete projects. My advice to him was to create balance with all the elements in order to achieve his goal. He took a compass reading to see where each room fell, and from there he observed how he had been charging up all areas of his home. (See Chapters 6 and 7 for more information on how to take compass readings in your home or office.) When he worked with the idea of balance he found he became very centered and much more relaxed. The tree element was no longer the predominant element in the home. Interestingly enough, he made a correlation with balancing the elements when he remembered that when he had lived at home with his mother, who had many bright paintings and earthy fabrics around, he had felt very low-key and less scattered. He then brought the same kind of balance to his own home.

Everything is alive and interacts with your energy—you deserve to have your home be your sanctuary. Look at what you want to achieve and use your surroundings to support your goals.

Quick Tips

- Clear out anything that does not serve you. A woman who heard me say this at a conference responded, "Easy for you to say!" She expressed how difficult she thought it would be. She was judging herself about what she should or should not do. Feng Shui is not about making your life more difficult, it is about checking in with what makes you feel alive and inspired. No judging allowed! Have fun and see this exercise as one that will start a domino effect. Your intention alone will bring amazing things into your awareness. I get e-mail all the time from people who have cleared out their homes and say, "Wow I feel great, what a shift in my energy," and, "I'm able to move past old patterns that were not serving me."

perky **Pictures** *and magic* **Mirrors**

Once you have chosen supportive colors for each room, you can begin to evaluate what kind of pictures and paintings work well in the space. Imagine the wall as a canvas. Remember that every time you walk by a painting, photograph, or other wall decoration, it makes an impression on your subconscious and interacts with you on an energetic level. If, for example, you see your "to do" list hanging in the kitchen first thing in the morning, you will be tempted to begin your mental churning before you have even begun breakfast. Consider carefully the mood of paintings.

Ask yourself, What do I want people to feel when they walk by this painting? Are the colors and themes supportive?

Do you have a lot of pictures that are deep, dark, and have an alone feel? A lot of individuals, especially eight-earth individuals, choose pictures that show one person in a desolate setting. Sometimes they can be introspective and uplifting, but other times isolating and depressing. One couple had pictures throughout their home of ships and of roads going off into the horizon. We all got a good laugh over the fact that the husband often spent ten months at a time overseas, away from home. Every picture was related to travel, either with no one in the photo or with someone alone. They all were beautiful, but they definitely depicted their situation. I suggested they put up more community-oriented pictures to enhance the family's harmony within the home.

Pictures set the tone

A travel agent I know had asked me to come in to give her suggestions in her business. She had a lot of clients but didn't seem to close all the deals she thought she should have. Often the clients would come in and totally fog out—their attention drifting to a faraway place. She would feel the rapport slip from the room.

Upon entering her office, I immediately noticed the picture she had hung over the desk. She loved it, but it was a dark painting that gave off a looming, scary feeling. When clients sat discussing their travel plans with her, they looked directly at the picture. It didn't give off a warm, fuzzy feeling, and didn't support her goal of booking clients on fun-filled vacations. I suggested she move the picture so she could see it, and put a lively travel picture behind her that would stimulate the client's sub-conscious to feel excited about fun and travel.

What you see is what you get

A client called who wanted to support his relationships through Feng Shui. He had a lot of paintings of Chinese swordsmen and war scenes in the most nurturing area (southwest) in his house. He found that

Remember that every time you walk by a painting, photograph, or other wall decoration, it makes an impression on your subconscious and interacts with you on an energetic level.

many times his employer, wife, and family members were receptive and friendly one minute, back-stabbing and aggressive the next. It is not that the pictures caused this to happen, but that they were a reflection of what was going on in his life.

I suggested photos of family members together, as well as scenes of people enjoying each other's company. He called after a few weeks of replacing his pictures and told me he had had a revelation that the aggressive behavior toward him was in response to how he interacted with others. He realized he was continually reactive and confrontational and he knew he was responsible for the underlying sword fighting with those he loved. This realization began a domino effect, and he became aware of his role in all of his relationships.

He was able to relax more when he focused on the new photos. This is not to say that the Chinese sword fighters were "bad," but in his case, changing the pictures helped him to see how he was reacting in his close relationships.

Brighter nights

Another couple's house was quite cheery but the walls were covered with very dark, sad, and lonely pictures of people in chains and ghostly faces—spooky, to say the least. Above their bed was a picture of a bleeding man. I had reservations about asking them where they got their art, but I had to find out if they enjoyed it. Their son, who had suffered from severe depression, had painted these pictures back in school fifteen years earlier. They had felt obligated to hang them. The son was now happy, feeling great, and felt he had passed through that stage and didn't want the pictures.

After I explained that this was their sanctuary and that perhaps a bloody man over their bed might not be the most romantic "over-the-bed item," they began to connect quite a few things that gave them a new perspective. We worked extensively in their bedroom because they had told me the spark had left their relationship. The wife read in the bedroom and had become introspective there.

The pictures you choose often reflect what is going on in your life.

We transformed the bedroom into a love nest with a new bed placement, a supportive, nurturing color for the wall, and upward lighting. We focused on the art that represented their relationship and on other issues they wanted to address. Two weeks after removing the pictures and working with the other suggestions, the wife called to say she felt like a new woman. She released the feeling of being responsible, which had kept her from living her life. She had freed up her relationship with her husband and her son, and a domino effect had started with all her other relationships. She saw that looking at the depressing pictures every day had put her into a downward spiral. She felt so much better that she came off the antidepressants she had been taking.

Evaluating your possessions

Your sanctuary is a place to keep your valued possessions—items that inspire and support you.

Your sanctuary is a place to keep your valued possessions—items that inspire and support you. Photographs of happy memories remind you of your loved ones, travel mementos bring back relaxing vacation images and works of art inspire your creativity. It is important to take a close look at your belongings, see what they represent to you and how they feel in your space. Do you get a warm, fuzzy feeling when you look at each thing in your space?

Reflections of relationships: Photographs

When I talk about this subject in my classes, people often have sudden revelations about items in their house that they feel don't fully serve them. One woman's father had been a pro football player, and he died when she was forty years old. Before his death she didn't have his picture around the house because at that time he represented authority to her and he constantly was telling her how to run her life. While she regarded him in an authority role, she felt best talking to him by phone, and not looking at his picture around the house. She didn't need to have him in her sanctuary because she didn't feel supported by him. So seeing his picture would only accentuate her lack of self-esteem. She had photos of the family having fun, but none of just him. She loved her father, but she couldn't see him as his own person until she worked on her self-image.

His death gave her the opportunity to rework her perception of him, and when she had accepted him fully, she was happy to put his pictures in the spotlight all around her house. Her kids loved the nostalgia. Because she had come to peace with him and the part of herself that felt judged, she was able to remember his positive traits. When she saw his picture on the wall she would giggle and remember his sense of humor and his "star-like" personality.

I often ask people what their photos or pictures mean to them. Go around and ask yourself, "What feeling do I get when I'm near this photo or picture?" Listen carefully to your internal response and the different layers to your reaction. Be careful about "should" statements such as, "I should love this picture because it's from my best friend's wedding." You will usually find a deeper layer of truth beneath them.

Mirror, mirror on the wall

Mirrors are often used in Feng Shui for a variety of reasons. They can expand a narrow hallway or draw sunlight into a dark room. I find mirrors to be spectacular for long alley kitchens and spaces that need to draw in natural sunlight. Amazing things happen when you use a mirror that effectively pulls in the outdoors and warmth from the sun. But they can also have a negative impact.

One woman in Florida called me because she felt invaded by relatives and surprise guests every other week. Tired of all the activity and wanting to be alone, she stopped answering her phone. It turned out that a few weeks after she had moved in, she had installed a whole wall, ten feet, of small strip mirrors about nine inches wide by five feet. The mirrors reflected the highway in front of her house. After the third week of living there, she developed heart problems and multiple panic attacks. The doctors told her she was headed for a nervous breakdown and that she may have had a mild heart attack.

When I sat across from her in her living room, it felt like the highway was driving through her living room. It was so unsettling and strange to be talking with cars flying and swerving around in front of me in her

Mirrors are often used in Feng Shui for a variety of reasons. They can expand a narrow hallway or draw sunlight into a dark room.

sanctuary. Worse than that, the small mirrors made the images vibrate and distort. Her nervous system would have had to shake after looking at those images day in and out. At night the lights were even more invasive. It was a spaceship-landing effect. It also was weird that as we were talking about this, she began to laugh, and said the overwhelmed feeling she had about her relatives dropping in, literally driving right into her space, was exactly the feeling the mirror gave off—everyone was invading her space. The driving-her-crazy feeling left soon after the mirrors were taken out. She called and told me that she couldn't believe that her home could feel so different without the traffic in her home. She said her sense of humor and sanity had been restored.

Mirrors are powerful and not to be taken lightly. Small mirrors can cause distortion and they often chop up an image. A mirror is ideal when you can see yourself clearly in it. It is the only time you see yourself, and it is best that it be a true reflection. A mirror that encompasses more than just a bit of an image, in other words a full picture, reflects balance and allows the brain to integrate.

Full reflection

One couple contacted me for a consultation. The husband felt that his efforts were going unnoticed at work. During the tour of their home, I noticed the mirrors were all very old and cracked, and hung very low. When asked why the mirrors were hung so low, the wife said that because she was shorter than her six-foot-five-inch husband, she assumed he could bend down to see himself in the mirrors set for her height. The problem was that he never did bend down, and energetically every mirror cut his head off; thus he never saw his own true reflection. Even in the morning while shaving, he was all scrunched over in a distorted kind of way. On a subconscious level he was reinforcing that his voice was not being heard, as if he were seen but not heard. They installed new mirrors. On some level he really did want to look in a clear mirror in the morning, and to his surprise he found that the new mirror that encompassed the whole upper half of his body helped him feel more integrated. He laughed to think he had taken on the crackled appearance that had reflected

Mirrors are powerful and not to be taken lightly. A mirror is ideal when you can see yourself clearly in it.

back at him every morning and that he could now see if his tie matched his shirt. He was happy to see he didn't have some of the wrinkles that the old mirror had reflected.

Timeless reflections

Have you ever walked by a mirror and felt spooked, as if you had seen a ghost? Well, certain arrangements of mirrors can be shocking. For example, two mirrors placed on opposite walls facing each other can be disconcerting and make you feel ungrounded, because when you look in the mirror you could see your reflection ad infinitum. This tends to bring up insecurities, as well as ancestral memories. I saw this at work at a bed-and-breakfast inn owned by a therapist. In her bathroom she had two large mirrors facing each other, which created a whirlwind and activated the guests' subconscious issues. The owner loved that because she felt that people visited her inn so that they could process and clear out their subconscious. All I could say was, "Yeah!" It was quite a combo platter of energies flying around to clear out.

Quick Tips

- Pictures and mirrors have a powerful effect on your well-being.

- It is best to able to see yourself clearly in all mirrors.

- Pictures have a psychological effect on your subconscious.

Pictures and mirrors have a powerful effect on your well-being.

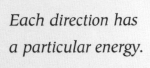

*Each direction has
a particular energy.*

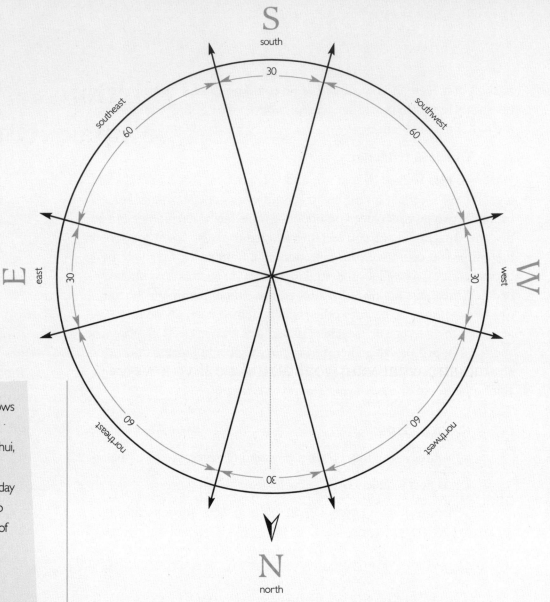

Notice that the diagram shows the south where north is traditionally found. In Feng Shui, the south represents the highest, hottest part of the day and thus is placed at the top to represent the high point of the energetic cycle.

living in the **Rhythm***:*
the **Compass Directions**

Imagine what your goal would be if you were buying or building a home. Would you search for a home with a southern exposure to take advantage of the added sunlight and the solar-heating effects? Or would you focus on finding a home with a westerly view to take advantage of the sun setting over the mountains? In either case you instinctively know that the compass directions are directly related to the rhythms of nature, just as the natural cycles are related to the Five Elements. Each direction has a particular energy. For example, the south is active and shines like the noonday sun—a time when you might want to be out in the world, while the north is calm and reflective—a time when you would want to be quiet and study. As you read this chapter, you will become more familiar with these energies and how they affect you in your home and office.

Supporting your goals with the compass directions

There are many ways to support your goals when working with the compass directions. Many homes and workplaces that feel dark are positioned so that they lack direct sunlight. How a home sits on a property makes all the difference in how you feel in each part of your home. Taking a closer look at how the sun moves around your home or office can give you insights into which parts are energized first thing in the morning and which parts get the sun in its setting stage, the afternoon. Just thinking about how you love the sun entering your kitchen in the morning, or that you hardly get any sunlight at all, is a start at looking at your home or office as a whole.

Each compass direction has a quality and a feeling to it, and the goal is to observe how the home as a whole affects your energy level. Using the compass directions also helps you with questions such as how to position beds and desks for maximum rest and productivity. Combined with your Nine Star Ki chart, they aid you in supporting each member of your family or office staff.

The compass directions in your home

The compass directions have a powerful effect on the energy flow in a space. Take a walk through your home and notice how you feel in each area. Is there a place where you like to read and relax? Are there rooms where you feel highly charged or able to focus on business and doing paperwork? Some parts of a home are a natural for a bedroom—just right for rest and recharging. Other parts are great for productivity. Many of my clients say they can't get a thing done in their home office, but if they sit at the kitchen table they have no problem getting caught up.

See how you feel in each room and then notice the qualities of the room. Why do you feel the way you do? Think of the many influences—the color, sunlight, energetic qualities, floor plan, or furniture.

It may be the floor plan, it may be the warmth of a room, or it could be how much sunlight enters the room; but the most important thing is that you begin to notice these different effects. Oftentimes it isn't the person or the space as much as it's the way the person's energetic system interfaces with the space. Each person and space is unique.

The qualities of the directions

As I mentioned, each direction has different qualities. They are described in the list below:

North fluid, adaptable, deep, activates the subconscious, dreams, and vision

Northeast introspective, inner knowledge, transformative

East active, upward-moving energy, new ideas

Southeast philosophical, creative, disseminating

South most active, expanding, full sun, illuminating, networking

Southwest nurturing, supportive, calming, social, family

West harvest, relaxing, tranquil, reflective

Northwest direct, focused, responsible

Position beds and desks for maximum rest and productivity.

How to read the directions in your home or office

1. Draw your house plan on a piece of graph paper. (Use an architectural floor plan if you have one.) Measure the outside walls with a measuring tape for the outside dimensions of the home. Next measure each room and draw it as it fits into the whole. Be sure to include extensions and areas where the walls indent.

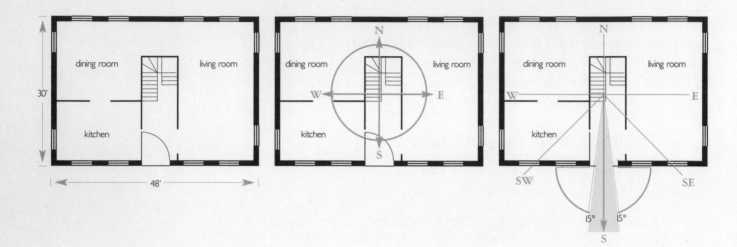

The front door is considered to be the door that the architect planned to be the front door of your home, even if you use another door more frequently.

2. Take a compass direction at your front door as you stand looking out the door. Make sure there are no metal objects nearby that can throw off your reading. The reading should be exact. The direction you are facing is the direction your home or office faces.

3. Take the diagram and line up the front door direction with its corresponding direction on the chart. Now drop the diagram onto the floor plan. Notice that south, west, north, and east have thirty degrees and the southwest, northwest, southeast, and northeast have sixty degrees.

4. Now find the center of the home with a ruler by drawing a line from the top to bottom on the diagram, then from side to side. Where the two lines intersect is the center point. (If you have a L-shaped house, for example, complete the shape with a dotted line so you have a square. Then find the center point of the home, which may fall slightly outside the actual walls. This might sound odd, but you are finding the energetic center. For more on non-square houses see Chapter 7.)

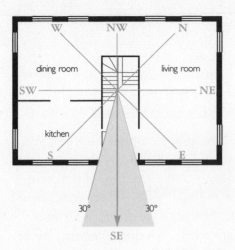

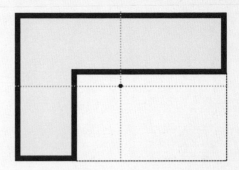

5. Using a protractor (some compasses also have degree markings on them), draw a line from the center point of your home to the outside wall in each direction. For example, say you are defining the south. You would draw a line from the center point of your home to ninety degrees, which is the middle of the south direction. Then measure fifteen degrees in either direction on the protractor. You would draw two lines, one to the left and the other to the right. This creates a thirty-degree, pie-shaped sector for the south.

For example, if your home faces southeast you would align the front door with southeast on the diagram. Once you have established the direction of your front door, you can then distinguish which directions the other rooms face and which sectors they are in.

The compass directions and the trigrams

In Chapter 2 we discussed how the natural cycles are represented by eight trigrams of the *I Ching*. Each of these trigrams also represents a compass direction. So, every direction has a trigram associated with it.

Think of the natural qualities of the directions. Compare the North Pole, where there is ice and snow, with southern Florida, where the sun burns your skin. Each has a unique feeling and quality. Or think of the cycle as following the sun, actively rising in the east, setting in the west, then moving to the midnight stillness of the north. These qualities are also represented by the trigrams, which are helpful for understanding the archetypal energy behind the directions. The trigrams and the characteristics for each direction are outlined and described in the following section.

Each compass direction has a unique feeling and quality.

North   *The trigram* **Water**

Northeast   *The trigram* **Mountain**

East   *The trigram* **Thunder**

Southeast   *The trigram* **Wind**

South   *The trigram Fire*

Southwest   *The trigram Earth*

West   *The trigram Lake*

Northwest   *The trigram Heaven*

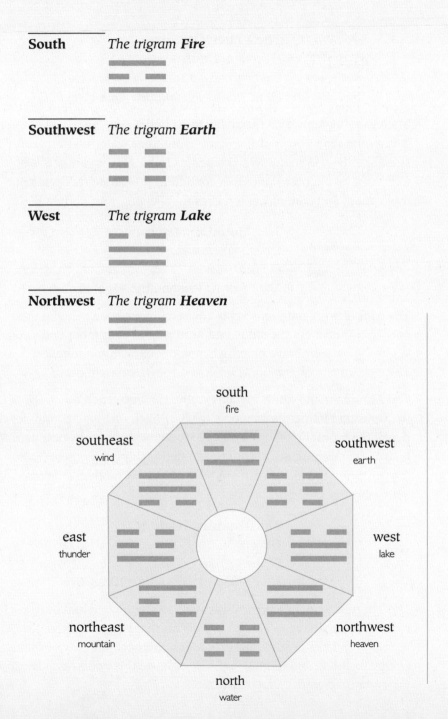

The trigrams represent the archetypal energy of each direction.

The Water Trigram

Direction: North
Element: Water
Nine Star Ki Personality: One-Water

The Water trigram offers the ability to be in the flow. Also, you can view it from the perspective of the many forms that water takes: ocean, lake, stream, or bog. Water moves and adapts to its surroundings. It is able to expand to the boundaries that contain it. It is about independence, motivation, and endurance. It relates to following your path in life.

The Mountain Trigram

Direction: Northeast
Element: Earth
Nine Star Ki Personality: Eight-Earth

The Mountain trigram represents stillness, inner knowing, and intro-spection. It is about the study and nurturing of your inner knowledge. It represents your "cave time," when you look within and reflect. Through inner exploration, change and transformation occur.

The more we know ourselves (Mountain trigram), the more we are able to be in relationship with others (Earth trigram).

The Mountain and Earth trigrams counterbalance each other. (Notice their position in the diagram on page 57.) Each one is important for the development of the other. The more we know ourselves (Mountain tri-gram), the more we are able to be in relationship with others (Earth trigram). And the more we are in relationship with others, the more we learn about ourselves.

The Thunder Trigram

Direction: East
Element: Tree
Nine Star Ki Personality: Three-Tree

The Thunder trigram represents actively rising upward and bursting forth. It is the ability to act on your vision that you glean from the Water trigram. It relates to sprouting new ideas and beginnings, springtime energy, building and formulating. You can see this energy manifesting in the expansive growth of a new company.

The Wind Trigram
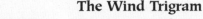
Direction: Southeast
Element: Tree
Nine Star Ki Personality: Four-Tree

The Wind trigram represents the airflow that distributes the seeds that spread growth and replenish the earth. Wind circles the world and expands your abundance. Abundance can be related to wealth, but abundance encompasses so much more than simply how much money you have. The Wind trigram is also about travel, exploration, and continual learning.

The Fire Trigram

Direction: South
Element: Fire
Nine Star Ki Personality: Nine-Fire

The Fire trigram represents social interaction, spreading of ideas, networking, inspiration, and being able to be recognized for who you are. It can be about being in the public eye. It is the warmth of the sun and passion that inspires us. It is expanding, illuminating, and expressive.

It is the warmth of the sun and passion that inspires us.

The Earth Trigram

Direction: Southwest
Element: Earth
Nine Star Ki Personality: Two-Earth

The Earth trigram represents the receptive; it is the most feminine and nurturing trigram. The Mother Earth supports us. It is our home, where we get the nutrients we need to survive. It is about being in relationships with others. The Earth trigram also represents gathering of information. This trigram represents the ability to settle down, become calm, and restore our energy.

People who are worn down and get burned out easily may need to strengthen the Earth element in their home.

The Lake Trigram

Direction: West
Element: Metal
Nine Star Ki Personality: Seven-Metal

The Lake trigram represents a calm surface, with activity stirring underneath. It signifies the joy in our life and the time of harvest. This trigram is about enjoying yourself, having fun, and rewarding yourself for your efforts.

The Heaven Trigram

Direction: Northwest
Element: Metal
Nine Star Ki Personality: Six-Metal

The Heaven trigram represents the male creative energy, wisdom, and clarity, as well as the ability to complete projects. It is about getting the support you need. The Heaven trigram represents getting things done and moving on.

In the next chapter on house shapes and flow, as well as in each of the remaining chapters, I will go into some experiences people have had working with these principles. Take the time to use the tools from this chapter to explore your living and working spaces. Then as you read, see what might work to improve or change these spaces. Remember, let these tools help you, but let your intuition lead you!

The Heaven trigram represents the male creative energy, wisdom, and clarity.

happy **House Shapes**:
seeking wholeness

The most important factor in sizing up a home is to get a good feeling of the space. Does it make you feel expansive and open, or does it make you feel cozy and private—and which of those feelings makes you feel most at home? Some people gravitate to homes with a light and airy feel, and some people need a more grounded feel. It all depends on the person.

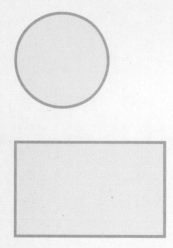

The overall shape of your home can dictate how well the floor plan flows. Many square or round houses have good circulation.

The overall shape of your home can dictate how well the floor plan flows from one room to the next, and can have a profound impact on your peace of mind. Take a look at your floor plan to see how one part of the house flows to another. For example, does the floor plan move in a circle from one room to the next, or does it perhaps have one hallway with rooms branching off of it? When you walk into your home are there several directions you can take? Once inside the house is there more than one way to get from room to room? Do you have to walk through several rooms to get from one end of the house to the other? Does your house have wings that dead-end? Are there long, narrow hallways? All of these questions will help you decipher the flow of your home. Then you can move toward creating what you want to achieve.

House shapes

Many square or round houses have good circulation because they have depth, promote ease of movement, and have good access throughout. On the other hand, homes that are L-shaped with the vertical leg either on the left or the right create one-way traffic. To get from one end to the other you have to traverse the entire length. This is particularly common with old renovated farmhouses. This shape may limit your options. If you live in a space like this, see how it feels to you. Following are stories about augmenting the flow in this kind of space.

An L shape may manifest as a lack of close family relationships. This shape lacks fullness and wholeness, and can create the feeling that there is no inner sanctuary.

One woman who lived in an L-shaped home avoided one part of her house because it was a long hallway energetically, and she felt it was wasted space. She had the home on the market to sell and no one wanted it. Every prospective buyer would come in, walk around quickly, and then leave. Many commented that the house's L-shape felt too exposed to the outside.

I told her that if we expanded the space energetically it would help sell the home. We began by making the entry more inviting. She made many alterations through lighting, painting, and the creation of a more circular flow in the home. She used mirrors in areas to widen the rooms that were long and narrow. By the time she was done, she decided she liked the changes. The house was in a really great neighborhood, and she decided to stay. She built a greenhouse porch room, which gave a new expansive shape to her home. She felt as if the house took on a new feeling, with better flow and circulation, as well as access to the whole home.

Many Florida homes are L-shaped with a pool in the middle. Everyone has access to the pool and it is a central place to gather. In this situation the middle becomes part of the house energetically. Like an atrium or gathering space, it changes the feeling of the home. Sometimes this creates a U-shape, which may be overwhelming to live in for some people because of the lack of circulation and flow. Each home is different. Don't look at a home shape as good or bad, think about how it feels to you and whether it supports your needs.

Additions or extensions

Looking at the floor plan of your home, you may notice that you have an addition or extension. An extension is an area that measures less than 50 percent of the full length of the wall that it's on. If you have an extension you may notice that you have added support in that area of your life. For example, you may have an extension in the east and feel that you have extra creative energy to explore and initiate new projects. Or the added tree energy from the east could be overstimulating for you. The influence of an extension will vary greatly, depending on the overall flow in the home, the directions, you, and myriad other influences.

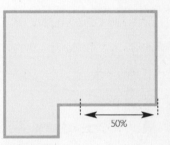

Extension

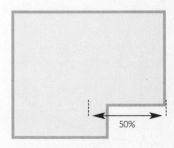

Not an extension

North	fluid, adaptable, deep, activates the subconscious, dreams, and vision
Northeast	introspective, inner knowledge, transformative
East	active, upward-moving energy, new ideas
Southeast	philosophical, creative, disseminating
South	most active, expanding, full sun, illuminating, networking

Southwest   nurturing, supportive, calming, social, family

West   harvest, relaxing, tranquil, reflective

Northwest   direct, focused, responsible

You will notice that the southwest is the most feminine and nurturing because its trigram is the Mother Earth, receptive and calming. The northwest is the most masculine; the trigram is heaven, fatherly—the opposite of the earth.

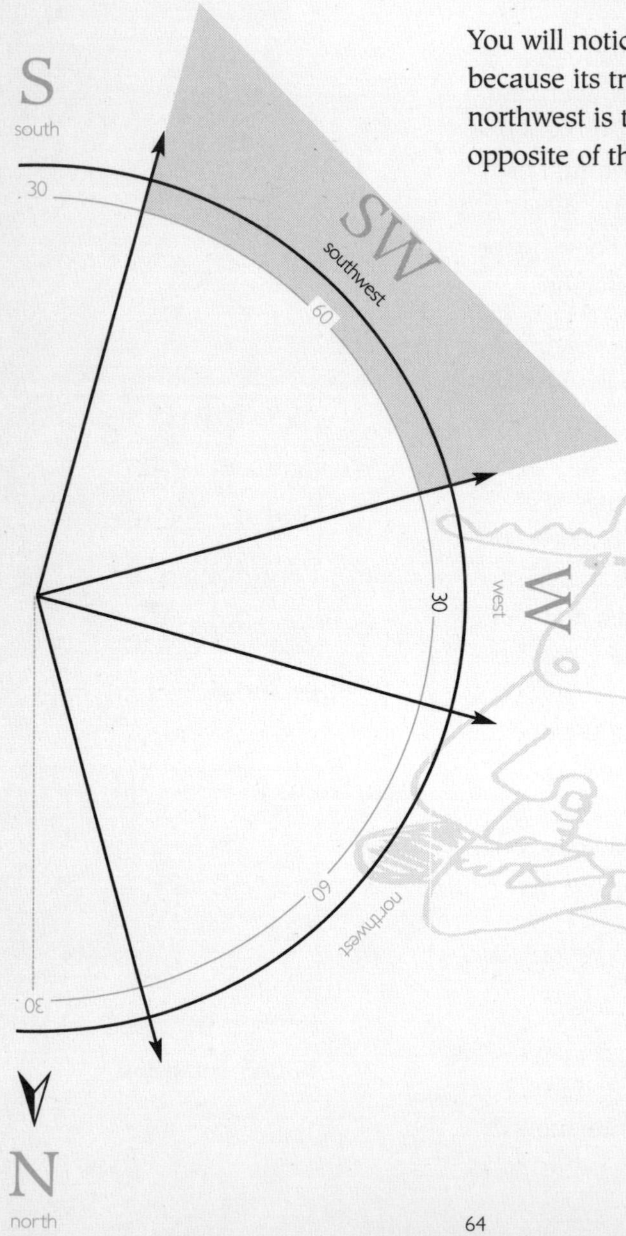

S
south

30

SW
southwest

60

30

west
W

30

60

northwest

30

N
north

How the energy flows in your home

Look at your floor plan; notice which direction the front door faces. It may give you insight about the overall energetic of your home. It may be facing east, getting the first hit of the morning sun. Then most likely your home is active and energized. Depending on other factors, such as the Nine Star Ki elements of the family members and the flow pattern in the house, you may experience the direction influence in different ways.

After you have determined the direction of the front door, look to see what direction your rooms fall in. For example, does your living room face the southeast, as well as your front door? You can refer back to the Five Elements in Chapter 2 or 4 to read about the east and southeast directions. You may also want to refer to the Nine Star Ki Appendix to see how your personal chart fits in the overall picture. For example, if you are a nine-fire personality, the southeast house direction may support your personal chart, while if you are a two-earth personality, you might feel the home is too active.

Rooms

Some rooms naturally support being able to resolve problems. They promote calmness and receptivity. Take note of the places you gravitate to in your home. See where you kick back and read the paper or rest— notice the colors in that part of the house. All homes have some areas that are more energized and conducive to getting things done, and others that are better for resting.

One woman asked me which bedroom in her mansion would be the best to sleep in to support her in her new relationship. She was a six-metal personality, so the earth directions best support her (because the earth element supports metal). Southwest would best support a romantic relationship, plus a restful night's sleep. Northeast would be more focused on introspection and inner knowledge.

Another woman felt her house was so still and quiet, she couldn't get any business done. She had a northeast front door, plus her office was in the northeast, the most contemplative spot in the home. She moved her office into the southeast to see how that felt, and found she had more

The front door is considered to be the door that the architect planned to be the front door of your home, even if you use another door more frequently.

ideas and more energy. She finally ended up in the northwest because that is where she felt grounded and able to do business and have the stamina to work through the day. She also noticed that the people she was in partnership with through the Internet seem to be more in line with her goals.

Quick **Tips**

■ The goal in your home is to feel that it is a true expression of who you are. If you'd make changes in your home, what would they be and why? Maybe it's that you don't like a certain room because you have the heating pipes running through it, making the ceiling two different heights. Maybe you've outgrown the size of your home. Whatever feelings you have, it's worth looking deeper. Sometimes the surface feeling is attached to something deeper that you can work with when it's clearly identified.

■ This is intellectual information, so check in with your intuition and see what aspects of your life feel great and which areas you'd like more support with. Then look at the shape of your home and the directions to determine if there is a correlation. More often than not, you'll see some kind of connection with your energy levels, as well as your overall well-being. If these areas are already strong for you then you won't be drawn to change anything. Listen to your intuition! Feng Shui is not about giving dos and don'ts. I love stories and how they allow you to make correlations in your own life. Create, have fun, and play around with the ideas to see what feels best for you.

Many influences can affect how you feel in a space. Checking in with your intuition as you play around with these ideas is the best way to get insights that support your goals.

enlivened **Entryways**

Hotels are great examples of what an entryway can do for a building. Most people have seen a hotel that has a beautiful, extended entryway with ground lighting along the path and shrubs leading up to the building. Often there is a fountain or a fishpond that is lit, or a defined garden greeting you as you walk up to the door. Hotels that have spectacular entryways help guests decompress even before they've reached the front desk. Psychologically, the guests leave the hectic world behind and begin to relax. This intention is felt as you enter the driveway.

If your entryway has a similar effect, you will be put into a relaxed state the minute you turn into your driveway or apartment complex. Your body will have the memory of home being related to a relaxed state, and the driveway will trigger the response. Each segment of the approach has a different effect on how you psychologically unfold and let go of the layers of your day. When you approach the entryway to your home and then open your door, you ought to have the feeling that says, "Ah, I'm home." The entryway is the area that greets you after a long day. It should bring a smile to your face.

The approach to your place

Driveways

In evaluating your entryway, start with your driveway or the approach to the house. Your driveway begins the journey up to the home. If you live in an apartment complex or you are evaluating your business, consider the drive or walk up to your building as your driveway.

Driveways that are widest where they meet the road and curve outward make it easy to enter from both directions.

Picture your driveway. As you drive up, evaluate if there is easy access in and out of it. Is it clearly marked? Do friends find it with ease? Do you get excited about the thought of being home? Driveways that are widest where they meet the road and curve outward make it easy to enter from both directions. Circular driveways are wonderful for allowing circulation and flow. Ask yourself if you can park easily and get to the path that leads you into your sanctuary.

The path leading up to the house from your driveway is extremely important. Optimally it is complete, well lit, and defined clearly from the driveway up to the door. If you are in an apartment or a home that is close to the road, evaluate what your comfort level is. Do you feel the parking area is adequate and comfortable to get into your home? Observe how you feel. Some people are perfectly happy being next to a road, while others feel vulnerable and invaded.

Lighting: Feeling safe and welcomed

Ground uplighting can do wonders for an entryway. Think of trick-or-treating as a child—remember all those poorly lit walkways? A well-lit entryway feels safe and inviting. This is not to say you should install blinding spotlights. Uplifting, soft, and illuminating lighting can distinctly indicate the path to your home, your porch, and front door. A person walking or driving up to your home will feel more at ease when they are able to see easily and clearly where they need to go. If you live in a home that is hard to find and the lighting is poor, try adding a lighting system that clearly defines your home so it can be seen from the road. Small path lights, such as the upward-shining or dome types, are wonderful for warming up an entryway and expanding the home.

Creating outward expansion

When it is dark outside, people inside can feel exposed and closed in because others can see into the house but they cannot see out. When soft ground-lighting lights up the shrubs, path, and entry, it changes the feel dramatically: The outside is illuminated and the occupants can see out to the yard, expanding the space. We have all been to a building where Christmas lights have been used to light up a tree or outline a door. Often restaurants use lighting to illuminate the entryway, giving the feeling that the outdoors is a part of the restaurant.

Invisible neighbors

Illuminated and clearly defined entryways make a strong impression on your visitors and neighbors. One client called me with concern about her relationship with her neighbors. She felt isolated from the rest of her neighborhood, and no one ever made an attempt to visit her or wave to her as she drove by. When we were standing in the driveway, a neighbor walked by, smiled, stopped, and then asked, "Did you just move in?" My client turned to her and said, "No, I've lived here for five years." The neighbor said, "I would have never known by driving past that anyone lived here. Why don't you come over for coffee and we can visit." My client had her own question answered. The neighbors didn't talk to her,

Illuminated and clearly defined entryways make a strong impression on your visitors and neighbors.

not because they didn't want to know her, but because she had not created a welcoming feeling around her home. Her property also did not hold life force, so she was invisible to the world. The neighbors didn't recognize her when she drove by because they had no reference point with which to connect her.

On a deeper level this situation manifested in other areas of her life. She saw herself as undesirable to those around her and she projected that feeling onto the neighbors, who obviously didn't feel that way at all. Through outdoor lighting, a visible path to the door, trimming overhanging limbs, and the intention to greet the world in a new way, she became a part of the community.

Your impression on the world

A man who ran a large Fortune 500 company had a similar unwelcoming entryway, yet he absolutely disliked his neighbors and hoped they would never bother him. He asked me if it was important to have an entryway that was welcoming. I replied that it is possible to have a welcoming entryway and still create boundaries with the world. Think of a grand estate where there is a welcoming entryway. It's nice to arrive there, yet you don't feel you can honk your horn as you drive up. In essence, the entryway is a symbol of how you want to be seen in the world; it is the first impression someone has when they enter your property. Big doesn't mean better; work with what you have. Whether it is simple or grand, small or large, the intention behind your entryway is what counts and greets the world.

Up the steps

Picture the entire front of your home in relation to the entryway. Creating a stable, solid feeling up to the door is the goal. Many homes have front steps and railings that look as if they were an afterthought, simply stuck on the front. In these cases, small stairways that lead directly up to the door give the visitor an unsteady or "hard-to-get-your-groceries-in-the-door" feeling. Steps with open risers feel less secure than closed stone or brick risers. Closing in the risers and adding stone, slate, or lattice to fill in under the stairs will create a sense of support and stability.

Everything makes an impression

A client asked me if she thought a new mailbox with clearly marked numbers on it would help her sell her home. Certainly on a psychological level, a prospective buyer who is seeing your property for the first time is taking in the whole experience on a feeling level. Anything that gives them the feeling that the home is inviting, well kept and thought out can only add to their sense of well-being.

Look at your entryway

The following questions will help you decipher how your home's entryway relates to your life. The first thing you see as you return home influences how you feel. For example, if the first thing that greets you when you get inside the door is a picture of your husband's uncle Fred, and he makes you feel uneasy, what does that do to your energy level? These questions will help you evaluate the flow to the home, through the front door, and in the entryway. Take notice of what the next set of questions brings up for you.

- Ask yourself what the first thing is that happens to you when you walk through the door? Do you feel relaxed to be home or geared up?
- Notice where your focus goes as you walk through your front door. Do you look directly down a long hall?
- Are you welcomed by a warm, cozy living room?
- Are you quick to move to the kitchen to take care of unfinished business, such as returning phone calls or other chores?
- Is the first thing you see a picture of something that brings you into your heart? Is it something you picked up on a trip that reminds you of a great time you had? Or perhaps it's Aunt Sarah's old hat rack that you put in the entryway because you didn't know what to do with it. Is she someone you like?

Empowering entrances

In Feng Shui the front door is looked at as the gate, or the mouth through which nourishment, air, and life force enters the building. It is considered the transition area, the protective barrier before entering into your intimate space. In essence it's the interplay between the outside world and the inside space. It symbolically represents your boundaries—the defining border between the outer world and your sanctuary. Having an

Notice where your focus goes as you walk through your front door.

open entryway that's easy to move around in allows for maximum flow and definition between the entry and the rest of the home. When front doors open directly into living space, such as a living room or kitchen, you can experience an overburdening feeling because there is no clear transitional area. This can symbolize the outside world's encroachment on your personal life. It can also represent taking on too much responsibility. The following stories are about people who have had positive results when making adjustments to their entryways. Each story reflects how the occupants made a correlation between their entryway and aspects of their life.

The flow of creativity

A woman I have worked with over the past few years, who has amazing gifts and talents, called to discuss her problems at work. She worked for a firm that she felt didn't appreciate her, and if she could have found a new job she would have taken it. When I asked her what would make her happy, she told me her dream would be to have a part-time writing job where she could express her creativity, and be home with her new baby the rest of the time. Fear had kept her locked in to a job that brought her unhappiness.

A set-back doorway or overhang can make an entryway dark and hard to maneuver in.

Interestingly enough, her home reflected her situation. There was no foyer area in her home. Upon entering, you walked into a stairway and a hallway. A set-back doorway and overhang made it extremely dark and hard to maneuver in. She asked me if adding an entryway would help the overall flow in the home. I said, "Yes!" She designed a foyer area that extended eight feet from the front door to create a breezeway. This allowed the front door to be farther from the stairway and created a comfortable, well-lit entryway.

One day she went to work unaware that the builders would start construction on the project that day. When she arrived at work, a new understanding of her boundaries became clear to her. She found she had less tolerance for her boss, her job, and the relentless schedule. Around 10 A.M. she called home, only to find out they had ripped the door and frame off the front of the house. Her home construction was a reflection of what was going on for her emotionally. Before the construction, her entryway was congested and didn't support flow in the overall floor plan. She felt that as the new foyer unfolded and began to expand, so did her own creativity. The new entryway was open and created balance with the rest of the downstairs.

Her front door was located in the Water trigram (the north), which represented following her path in life. She was a five-earth/one-water, so any alterations to the front door area would affect her emotionally because the Water trigram of the front door lined up with her emotional number. She made major emotional shifts that led her to apply for a new job in a field she was more interested in. The new job came with ease and was perfect for expressing her talents. Also, her son was accepted into the day care she had been waiting two years for. She felt that she was in the flow and she was attracting things into her life that supported her.

Another couple had the same sort of entryway and all they did was move the door out two feet to allow for a bit more space. They added a skylight that brought natural lighting into the entryway, and it changed the whole energetic feel of the home.

Privacy

One woman had a set-back door that entered directly into her living area. She felt as though everyone could view her in her pajamas if she was in her living room. One day she was walking outside with her dog and her neighbor stopped to talk with her. As the two women were chatting she noticed the wind had caught the front door, and as the door swung open there stood her husband at the fridge in his undies. If it had been a side door it wouldn't have been so noticeable, but this was the front door. The neighbor waved at him and said, "Wow, I can see clear into your fridge from here." It was obvious to the couple that they needed to create a less-exposed entryway. They ended up putting a beautiful

The direction the front door faces influences how the home feels. A south-facing building gets direct sunlight and is an active building, compared to a north-facing door that has a more low-key feeling.

screen that curved around inside the entryway, separating the door from the rest of the home, giving more privacy.

North	fluid, adaptable, deep, activates the subconscious, dreams, and vision
Northeast	introspective, inner knowledge, transformative
East	active, upward-moving energy, new ideas
Southeast	philosophical, creative, disseminating
South	most active, expanding, full sun, illuminating, networking
Southwest	nurturing, supportive, calming, social, family
West	harvest, relaxing, tranquil, reflective
Northwest	direct, focused, responsible

What greets you as you walk in the door is so important. Is it your dog Sparky with slippers in his mouth, greeting you, and an entryway that welcomes you in to recharge you after your day?

Opening the front door: Inward flow

Once you have stepped up to the door and opened it, it is best if the door itself has as much space as possible to open. This holds true for both your home and your business. Being able to open the front door completely is preferable. Likely you have experienced a front entrance where the door opens to a wall perpendicular to the door, or a door that cannot fully open because a piece of furniture is in the way. In both of these situations you probably felt cramped; quite literally, there was not enough space to enter the home. This affects your guests. They may not know where to go; they may seem unsure where to put themselves. By contrast, large, open entryways allow for maximum circulation. Optimally, when you walk into an entry it is nice to have choices of rooms and directions to take once inside.

Open spaces

For example, one woman removed a coatrack from behind her front door so the door could move more freely. Her intention was to let in more light and more space to move around in the entryway. She noticed that the day she did this, beautiful sunlight streamed into the kitchen. The light had been blocked previously, and the changes made her feel more open and inspired to clear more areas in her home. The next morning she went to work with a chipper attitude; as she walked in, her boss commented on how good she looked and asked her if she would like to work on a new project that turned out to be very profitable.

Sometimes there are no obvious solutions for a tight, closed-in entryway. You can put your intention on expanding the space energetically and see what comes to you. Small things can make a big difference.

Optimizing entryways

Each person's situation is different. One man I know who worked at a computer firm had his desk behind the front door. The door actually opened directly to his desk, and the desk stopped the door from opening fully. After realizing he felt uncomfortable in that location, he moved out of the entryway. This allowed the door to open fully. His door, his gate to the world, was unblocked, and the inward flow was restored. More energy was able to enter the space. A day later he saw a change in his state of mind, and also saw his clientele and business steadily improve.

Often changing one small item can have a domino effect. It can open the flow of energy, which has to go somewhere. Science has proven that energy flows differently over different surfaces. For example, air flows over a round surface much differently than over a pointed surface, just as a deep-hulled boat moves through the water much differently than a rounded, shallow-bowed boat. Play around with your entryway. See how it feels to change the coatrack, or move the pile of recycling to the closet. Try some of the little things and notice the change they make in the energy flow into your home.

Science has proven that energy flows differently over different surfaces.

Quick **Tips**

The goal of the entryway is to be welcoming, easily accessible, grounded, solid, and supportive. Let's consider the basics:

- Is there a distinct, well-lit, and clear path leading to your door?
- Is it easy to get up the front steps to the front door?
- Is the entryway open enough for you and your guests to make the transition from outside to inside?
- See how the entryway makes you feel upon arriving home. Is it your castle?
- Intention is everything. Is the intention to create a warm, inviting home that offers instant comfort to those who enter?
- On a psychological level is there balance between the inner world and the outer world?
- Is there enough of a buffer zone?
- If it is a business, is the entryway inviting? Does it tell the story of what lies within? In other words, does it say, "This is a great place—come check it out!"

On a psychological level is there balance between the inner world and the outer world?

rejuvenating **Bedrooms**

renewing romance, rest, and relaxation

Bedrooms are the most intimate and personal places in your home. They are where you can go and get away to read, nap, exercise, recharge, and be intimate. If your home is your sanctuary from the rest of the world, your bedroom is your altar. It's worth taking the time to have the bedroom be a special place. Warm, cozy bedrooms can make all the difference in how well you sleep, rejuvenate after a long day, as well as support your intimate life.

To some, a bedroom is just a place where they go to sleep, and they would just as soon not open the door otherwise. Many people like their bedroom but feel something is missing. I'll go into a couple's bedroom and I'll ask them how well they sleep. Often the husband will speak up and say he sleeps great, but his wife does not, or vice versa. They might also relay that the spouse closest to the door wakes up easily.

A closer look

Take a closer look at your bedroom. Consider the next series of questions and see if anything strikes you.

- Is the bed in line with the doorway or tucked in a cozy spot?
- Is your bed directly on the wall near the door as you walk in?
- Is the bedroom off at the end of a long hallway?
- Are the ceilings filled with slanted angles?
- Are there beams over your head?
- Do you frequently wake unrested, even after a full night's sleep?
- Do you wake up late?
- Do you sleep restlessly or dream a lot?
- Does your bedroom make you feel nurtured and do you wake refreshed?
- Do you enjoy being in your bedroom?
- Is your bedroom a place where you can feel passionate?

There are a few key points to keep in mind in creating a bedroom that will allow you to awaken refreshed and at peace. I will cover color, bed orientation, and placement, as well as other ways to create the perfect bedroom for you. Keep in mind that each person responds differently to various arrangements and colors—let your intuition tell you what works best for you.

Bedrooms are the most intimate and personal places in your home.

78

Element	Water	Tree	Fire	Fire/Earth	Earth	Metal
Colors, shades of	blue black turquoise deep purples	green	orange-yellow yellow red bright yellows red-pinks	salmon peach pink	brown tan beige off-white with warmth	white gray silver metallics
Qualities	fluidity	movement new ideas	expansive charging	warm nurturing	grounding nurturing	clarifying defining
Supports	3-tree 4-tree 1-water	9-fire 3-tree 4-tree	9-fire 2-earth 5-earth 8-earth	2-earth 5-earth 8-earth 9-fire	6-metal 7-metal	1-water 6-metal 7-metal
Pulls off or settles	6, 7-metal	1-water	3, 4-tree	3, 4-tree	9-fire	2, 5, 8-earth

Color in the bedroom

One of the first elements to consider in your bedroom is color. What colors have you selected for your walls, bed linens, curtains, and furniture? Soft, warm tones are best because they make you feel supported and nurtured, and aid you in getting a restful night's sleep. Shades of yellow, soft pink, salmon, and warm off-white on the walls are grounding and calming. Most red shades can be overstimulating. Dark colors can sometimes be heavy and ponderous. White walls can be overstimulating and stark, accentuating mental activity. Some white walls are toned down when soft, light wood tones are a part of the space. Creating balance is the key. Dark wood tones combined with white often needs to be balanced with warmer colors. As I've mentioned before, color has a profound effect on your overall well-being.

The chart above describes the colors and their elemental qualities. Its purpose is to spark ideas and give you ways to create movement. Use it as a reference, but first trust your intuition. The chart is meant to open up possibilities, not to limit you. It doesn't imply that you shouldn't use a particular color. The message is, Play with color and see what it can do for you.

Changing patterns

A client of mine had chosen bold red wallpaper that was gorgeous and alive for her bedroom. As we talked, she made comments that indicated she and her spouse had a rocky relationship, and that she spent a lot of her time at home in their bedroom. She read in bed, she talked on the phone in bed, and the couple discussed their problems in bed before sleeping. This women spent a lot of her time in a room that was not only highly charged due to its southern location in the house, but was further amplified by the bold red color in the room. She realized that whenever she and her husband argued in the bedroom, he would quickly get hotheaded. He would then leave the room, unable to finish the conversation. The conflicts were always resolved in a room other than their bedroom, or even away from the house. They made a decision to talk over problems in another part of the house and also to paint the bedroom a calmer, cozier color to create balance. They noticed an immediate change. By becoming aware of the pattern, they could make changes to support their relationship.

Color for children's bedrooms

Everyone needs a sense of support and connection in their private rooms, but this is particularly important for young minds and hearts. It is preferable for a child's bedroom to be warm and nurturing. Shades of salmon, peach, and yellow that are earthy, not bright, work well. Warm, cheery beiges are supportive and will help a child feel secure. Greens and blues can be very supportive for some children, but it depends on the nature of the particular child. Use color as a balancing tool. For example, if a child needs to slow down a bit or if you need to help stimulate the child, you can use color to support your goal. Recently it has become popular to decorate children's rooms in bright, primary colors such as bold yellow, fire engine red, and royal blue combinations. The

It is preferable for a child's bedroom to be warm and nurturing.

thinking here is that they are stimulating colors, but in my opinion they are too stimulating for a bedroom. Remember, if the room is too stimulating it will be hard for children, especially young ones, to relax or focus on studies. You may also want to use blue sparingly, especially if your child is thoughtful and sensitive—too much blue can be depressing.

When choosing colors, think of your child's personality. Is he quiet and need a little bringing out? Then choose shades of yellow, salmon, or a light green. Is she bookish to an extreme? Then avoid white walls, which overstimulate the mental focus and could cause your child to become too analytical and withdrawn. White walls can also make it difficult for a child to get a good night's sleep. Many children love purple. Purple is the craze right now and can add spontaneity. Playing with color can be fun.

Creating balance is the key. See how you feel and what best supports you and your family. You may have a child who is very active and has a hard time getting to sleep. Your insights on your child's bedroom being in an active place in the house may be all you need to calm the room down with direction of bed placement, color, and Nine Star Ki information, which are discussed below. Play, have fun, and don't do anything that doesn't make you feel warm and fuzzy.

Cozy bedrooms

The part of the home the bedrooms are located in can affect how well family members sleep. Take, for example, a room that is located right by the front door. It can feel exposed because of being in the traffic flow. There isn't much privacy in a location that enters directly off of an entryway or a main family room. The direction the room faces can influence what a bedroom feels like as well. To establish what direction your bedrooms face, stand in the center of the home and take a compass reading. Note the qualities of the direction that influences each bedroom. (Use the floor plan diagram you drew in Chapter 7 to help you as well.) Each direction and part of the home has a different feel, and some bedrooms in your home may be more conducive to sleeping than others. Also, each person in your home may feel different in each

Play, have fun, and don't do anything that doesn't make you feel warm and fuzzy.

room. Once you have established how you feel in a room, you can think about the direction the head of the bed faces.

North	fluid, adaptable, deep, activates the subconscious, dreams, and vision
Northeast	introspective, inner knowledge, transformative
East	active, upward-moving energy, new ideas
Southeast	philosophical, creative, disseminating
South	most active, expanding, full sun, illuminating, networking
Southwest	nurturing, supportive, calming, social, family
West	harvest, relaxing, tranquil, reflective
Northwest	direct, focused, responsible

Although it may seem strange, try lying on the floor in the different directions in your room to feel the differences.

Bed orientation

Perhaps the next most important consideration is your bed, its location, and the materials from which it is made. Use a compass to find what direction the head of your bed faces. Each direction has a different feel and can affect the quality of your night's sleep. Beds with the head toward the north and the west will tend to encourage you to sleep deeply, much in the way that winter and evening make us more retiring and quiet. Those who choose to orient their beds with their head at the north or west may feel they have a deep, peaceful sleep, but may also have trouble waking up in the morning.

On the other hand, beds that are oriented toward the east or the south will encourage much more active sleep, but will also help those who need to get up early to rise with the sun! Of course, you can go into more detail; for example, a southwesterly bed orientation can be very nurturing and romantic for couples, whereas a northeasterly can be more introspective. Although it may seem strange, try lying on the floor in the different directions in your room to feel the differences. Many of my clients are amazed that they can feel the difference in the directions and how it affects their sleep.

Play around and see how you feel in the various directions. People have amazing results with bed orientation. Also, taking into consideration your Nine Star Ki chart can help you come up with what best supports you. First see how you feel in the different directions; then to give your mind more tangible information, look to see what your Nine Star Ki numbers and elements are, and see how the directions and your chart interact. Some directions may feel more supportive to you, depending on what your goal is. If your intention is to have a romantic, restful, cozy room, the southwest direction will probably feel supportive. If, for example, you are a six- or seven-metal, you most likely will feel good with your bedroom located in the southwest, because the southwest is of the earth element and earth supports metal. Again, it depends on your goal. So use the direction information once you have clarified your intention; and most important, see what feels best for you.

Finding the right direction for you

I suggested to a client who had not slept well in years to slightly change the direction of her bed to take advantage of a supportive direction. She had reservations about moving her bed because it was very heavy. She decided to first try sleeping in other rooms, which had beds facing in other directions. She found she slept like a baby in her son's room who was away at college. His room was in the northeast direction, which is the most still, introspective area in the home. Her own bedroom was in the southern direction in the home, the most active area. That alone could have influenced how well she slept at night. She then felt that a good night's sleep was possible, so she moved her bed from facing southeast to face the southwest, which made a big difference in how well she slept.

Your Nine Star Ki chart can help you come up with supportive directions.

Her son's room still felt better to her and she asked me why. Her Nine Star Ki numbers were (6,6), so the earth directions nurtured her, and her son's northeast room and southwest bed direction provided the perfect setup. Because her own room was in the southern part of the house, the fire element may have been too active for her all-metal Nine Star Ki chart.

Nothing is set in stone. You may not be able to move your bedrooms around, but if you are having trouble sleeping, try playing with the different directions to locate the best direction to support your energy level.

The north supports one-water, three-tree, and four-tree, as well as promotes dreamtime and deep sleep. The north can also calm six-metals and seven-metals. The north also supports a person who is a metal/tree combination because the water element bridges the metal and tree elements. Notice on the chart that the water element is in between the metal and tree elements.

Depending on what their intention is, other people may feel fine sleeping to the north. If you try this and still feel you are not sleeping well, you may be next tor the door or in an awkward area of the room.

The east and southeast support a three- or four-tree personality, as well as nine-fire. The east and southeast can support a nine-fire, because the tree element supports the fire element. These directions can support a one-water when the goal is to activate. The east and southeast are both of the tree element, yet will feel very different. Play around. For example, even if a person is a three- or four-tree, he or she still might feel best supported by the earthy, restful directions. That's why I stress over and over to check in with how you feel.

The south direction supports the nine-fire, and the two-, five-, and eight-earth personalities. The south (fire element) supports the earth element. The south also can be supportive for the three- and four-tree personality if the goal is to redirect. The south is an active direction and may not be the optimum choice for sleeping; but again, only you can find that out by experimenting.

If a person is a one-water/nine-fire, the tree element (east or southeast) will bridge the water and fire elements. Notice in the diagram that the tree element falls in between the water and fire elements.

One child constantly had nightmares and ended up in his mom's bed regularly. The whole family was dragging around in the mornings. The child slept with his head facing the north, which can be dream-activating, and he was a three-tree/two-earth. His mom changed his bed direction to the south (fire element) and he snoozed up a storm. The fire element bridged his Nine Star Ki elements. Notice in the chart that the fire element is in between the tree and earth elements.

The southwest and northeast directions support the two-, five-, and eight-earth personalities, as well as the six- and seven-metal personalities. (The earth element supports the metal element.) The southwest and northeast can be very helpful for a nine-fire person who may be too active or overheated. The calming earth direction settles down the fire energy. Anyone who has the tendency to overheat can find this useful. The southwest is a good direction for supporting romance and restful sleeping. The northeast is more sedate and contemplative. These directions can be settling for anyone who needs to calm down mentally or physically. These directions can also be great for people who are fire/metal combinations, as the earth bridges the fire and metal elements. Notice in the diagram that the earth element is in between the fire and metal elements.

Of course, each person will resonate to what is going on in their personal situation; for example, who else sleeps in the room and where the room is located in the home.

The west and northwest are supportive for six- and seven-metal personalities, as well as one-water personalities. It also can feel supportive for two-, five-, and eight-earth people who feel stagnant. If a person is a one-water/two-, five-, or eight-earth combination, the metal element (west, northwest) can bridge the water and earth elements. The northwest can be a mentally active direction and may not be settling enough, but try it out.

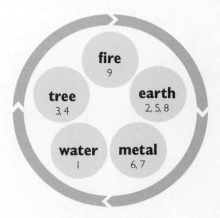

In deciding where to put your bed, also consider the room layout.

Bed placement

In deciding where to put your bed, also consider the room layout. Take a look at the spot where you are thinking of locating your bed. Will the headboard be on the same wall as the door? Will you be sleeping next to an entrance? These aspects are likely to disturb your sleep, particularly if your mate comes in after you have drifted off. Having the head of your bed under a beam, shelf, or a sloped ceiling may be associated with problems such as insomnia and headaches. It is not something to be fearful of, just see how you feel in each spot. Play around with several options.

One woman I worked with called specifically because she wanted validation as to why she had a hard time sleeping in her master bedroom. She had a skylight over her bed and the roof pitched toward the head of the bed. She felt as if a landslide were heading towards her head. I could experience exactly how she felt just by standing in the doorway to her room. The whole effect was one of instability. As we were talking we moved her bed to a different direction that was supportive for her, and she was amazed that she felt better instantly. She started sleeping in her room again, and felt better that her intuition had been validated.

Be choosy about your bedding. Select mattresses and beds that make you feel supported and comfortable. Bedding material can affect how well you sleep at night.

Air, light, and silence

Windows can also affect a room's atmosphere. Some people love sleeping under a window, while others feel exposed and insecure when not up against a wall. Fans and air circulation are other important considerations. Nothing is nicer then a beautiful breeze and fresh air at night while you sleep. An open window or fan in summer will circulate air, the softer the feeling, the better. Paddle fans are soft and feel cozy for a restful night's sleep. See what gives you a restful feeling.

Another element to keep in mind is the number and sound of electronic devices in your room. If you are finding it hard to fall asleep, it can be that your mind is too active. Some people find it preferable to keep televisions, computers, loud clocks, and phones out of the bedroom—these machines can disturb your sleep. Even small things can be annoying when you are trying to sleep.

Romance: Intimacy in the bedroom

Beyond your bed, other elements can profoundly impact you. For couples, especially newlyweds and those who want to enhance their relationship, it is especially important to create a sense of intimacy and togetherness. Is the furniture something you bought together, or was it handed down from your mother or grandmother? For couples, the bedroom is the place to have items that represent their relationship, such as pictures that are peaceful and meaningful.

Creating a supportive bedroom

One couple had their bed directly on the wall where the door opened into their bedroom. The room was small, and they were exposed because they were next to the stairway. Everyone in the house passed the room as they went up the stairs, which didn't allow for privacy for the couple. Their room really was part of the hallway. It was easy for them to say, "Oh it's okay, we are only in our room after everyone is in bed," but the bottom line for this couple was that they really didn't have a spot to be private and intimate.

Just by my bringing it up, they saw the necessity to create a place that allowed them to read at night, to snuggle if they wanted, and not be on the wall of the stairs where every little noise echoed in their room. That day they moved the bed to come out at an angle from a far wall and added a little table behind the bed for books and a light. They also painted the room a soft, romantic color and hung pictures they loved on the walls. Soft, big, cozy pillows added to the atmosphere, as if inviting them to come in and read.

These changes allowed them to have a place that was their own. Moving the bed made the room feel bigger and less like Grand Central Station. The direction their heads faced was southwest, which supported their individual charts as well as their relationship. Angling the bed also softened the room's shape, giving it a very romantic feel. The wife reported back that it totally changed the focus in the home. They made other related changes, working with uplifting lighting; and they painted other sections of the home as well. Small changes—huge results.

Small changes— huge results.

Another couple I consulted with had a bedroom with two entryways. The bedroom was actually en route to another room. A stairway opened into the bedroom through one door, and a hallway through the other. The home was long and thin with two stairways up to the second floor, and if both of the bedroom doors were open, their bedroom became a through-way. The home actually had a great floor plan for a large family and entertaining. It was their bedroom that needed a new plan.

The room did not lend itself to intimacy or even a good night's rest. The goal was to slow down the "hallway feeling" and create a love nest. The first thing was to close off the entry into the room from the back stairway by moving a large piece of furniture that had been in their closet in front of the door. The bedroom had large beams overhead and many angled walls. They added a false ceiling out of fabric. The husband said the big cloth helped create a cozy night's sleep. By using the material, they balanced the overabundance of wood in the room. They also made adjustments in the hallway outside the bedroom to slow the energy down.

Recharging bedrooms

Often long homes have long hallways that can lead to awkward bedroom layouts. I met a cute couple recently that had the best sense of humor. As I walked into their home I felt that they were a very speedy family. I knew the wife had tree and fire elements in her Nine Star Ki chart, so it would be imperative for her home to be a place where she could chill out after a long day. Their home had been on the market to sell and they had recently decided to take it off because it hadn't sold. The realtor had told them to add drawn curtains and keep the walls white—the entire home had white walls and dark wood. It was so white that it felt cold, and it had a stark feel because there were only a few pictures on the walls. Both the husband and the wife needed sunlight to enter the home, so I suggested they go back to what they liked, which was seeing a beautiful view of the outdoors.

Due to snoring, each had their own bedroom. The husband was Austrian and cute as can be, and the wife was Brazilian, I believe, expressive

Fire and tree personalities have upward-expanding energy. It is helpful if their home is settling and nurturing to help calm down their energy.

and equally cute. When I entered his bedroom I was hard-pressed to speak. It was a stark room with only a bed. The curtains were drawn with a blackening cloth, and a small ceiling light hung down with a long pull chain. I could just picture someone sitting below the light, hands tied behind his back, blindfolded, being interrogated—not a warm and fuzzy scenario. A minimalist one, for sure. When he saw my face he started to giggle and asked what I was thinking. I said that it reminded me of an interrogation room. He laughed.

He agreed that if it would slow down the energy in the home and help them restore needed balance, he would gladly warm up his room. The wife had read that adding colored objects above his door would make him feel good, so she had placed a red-colored Christmas bulb above the entryway to his room and office. She laughed when we noticed it, saying that it was the only color in the house, and we joked that she'd better leave it there. As we walked around the rest of the house, out of the blue he would laugh and say, "Hey, we can bring this down to the interrogation room to warm it up."

We talked about adding a warm-colored comforter and possibly a new light fixture that would add upward lighting to the room. The funny thing was that all the bedrooms had the "interrogation" lighting fixtures, but the daughter had hung horse pictures and school stuff from her light pulls—a fun look. Adding color to the rooms would help soften the stark shadows on the wall and settle down the energy.

The man had back problems, and we worked on opening up the hallways leading to the bedrooms. The restricted narrow hallways did not allow circulation and optimum flow to that part of the house. The emphasis was to create an overall plan that supported health, romance, optimum flow, and most of all, relaxation in all parts of the home. Using color and taking in the natural sunlight wherever possible was important, as well as opening up and expanding the central channel of the home with a floor-to-ceiling mirror placed in the long hallway. (Floor-to-ceiling mirrors, when in the right spot, can give the illusion that the wall behind has disappeared. Most people have no idea how profound the expansion can be until they do it.)

Floor-to-ceiling mirrors, when in the right spot, can give the illusion that the wall behind has disappeared.

Quick **Tips**

- Creating a warm, nurturing space to sleep and relax in is beneficial to your overall well-being.
- The bed and bedroom location can affect how well you sleep.
- The colors you choose can support a restful night's sleep.

The emphasis was to create an overall plan that supported health, romance, optimum flow, and most of all, relaxation in all parts of the home.

heartwarming **Home Offices**

Many individuals are choosing their home as their workplace. More and more people have the opportunity to work from their home and this has opened up all kinds of possibilities for work environments. Whether you are going to spend full days or just several hours on the weekend, the home office needs to support you and your goals.

How often is our home office a place to throw our bills, heap up our miscellaneous papers, or house our "to-do stuff"—staplers, penholders, paper clips, and overall "no-fun" things? It screams, "Don't come in! It's no fun!" Some of us have a favorite chair or piece of art in our office that we love, but more often than not the so-called office space is pretty official.

Having fun in the office

Subconsciously a "responsibility beeper" goes off in our head when we walk in the office. One couple I worked with had a great deal of concern about the husband's lack of ability to focus and get things done. His basement office had a cold, no-fun feeling. The good thing about it was that it let in daylight—it was an aboveground basement that had natural sunlight.

Warm fire colors support the earth element and two-, five-, and eight-earth personalities.

The husband was an eight-earth/two-earth, which meant warm colors and sunlight would support his overall goal. But the white walls drained his energy and accentuated his mental focus, so his mind was constantly active. The color they chose was a rich salmon that warmed the room and allowed him to stay more centered. He could work longer hours and felt more grounded.

To take advantage of the natural sunlight and expand the space, they added a floor-to-ceiling mirror, which pulled in the beautiful green trees from outside that could be viewed from his desk, so he felt like he was enjoying the outdoors in his office. The green reflection created movement and stimulation and enhanced his creativity. Eight-earth people can be very serious, and I suggested that every time he came downstairs he needed to make a funny face in the mirror. Of course his wife loved this recommendation, and he thought I was silly.

He knew from past experience with me that my suggestions usually brought some amazing changes, so he said he'd write himself a reminder note. This became a funny ritual that inspired the challenge to do a new face every time he passed. He also added fun pictures he loved to his office, along with a comfy chair that his wife could sit in and chat with him. The icing on the cake was that he loved salsa music, so his wife bought him a CD to listen to. The basement didn't feel like a basement anymore.

Desk placement

Desk placement in a home office is just as important as it is in an office building. Having the desk face out of the room with the worker's back to the wall keeps distractions to a minimum and allows the worker to be open to new ideas.

If clients come to your house, think about having your office near an outside door. If your office is in the basement, have a clear path to the door. It is good to consider what rooms you want people to walk through to get to the home office. It is nice to keep business situations from encroaching on your personal space if possible. Wherever the office is located, it is important that the entranceway be clearly designated to avoid any confusion on the part of the client.

Empowering choices

One client who was reorganizing his office space was a writer. He collected old magazines, and his office was filled with old cigar boxes, trinkets, and mementos of fond memories. We discussed getting rid of anything he didn't absolutely love. Many things were very special to him, but he had just as many things he was more than happy to let go of. We talked about what he wanted to achieve in the consultation and his main goals were as follows:

- To feel more empowered by his choices
- To be recognized for his talents and writing ability
- To stay ahead of his workload and have time for his family
- To have a business desk that he could sit at to do his bills
- To have his creative juices flow with ease
- To stop feeling overwhelmed

His office was a clear reflection of his concerns. He had three desks completely covered by piles of notes, bills, old phones, and non-office things; yet he had no place to really sit down and write on a clear surface.

Having fun is the theme. Feng Shui is about creating BALANCE, *so bring into your space anything that brings you a chuckle.*

There was an old fluorescent light he joked hadn't been washed off in twenty years. A few of his light fixtures blinked on and off.

His walls were a blue-white and had a glaring feel to them. I suggested he paint the walls a warm color that supported his Nine Star Ki personality, nine-fire/eight-earth. He chose a vibrant salmon color (a combination of the earth and fire elements) to help him feel active and enthused. Greens also would have supported his fire energy, but not his eight-earth emotional number. I suggested also adding upward lighting to lift the ceiling and soften the room.

Another recommendation was to clear out all non-writing office-related items. We then arranged his writing desk to face the southeast to support his creativity and writing, and his business desk to face the northwest to support paying bills and completing business. On the wall across from each desk we placed inspirational pictures that brought him into his heart and helped him remember to enjoy his work.

We added a mirror on a wall to draw in the view and natural lighting from outside.

We added a mirror on a wall to draw in the view and natural lighting from outside through a sliding door in the next room. The green from outside stimulated his creativity, and the mirror (the water element) supported his fluidity and spontaneity. Adding a picture of people enjoying themselves subconsciously helped him feel supported by family and friends.

Last but not least, we discussed what he had in his three filing cabinets. He told me that one set held all his business transactions, which were useful and needed to be nearby. The other one held old murder cases, which he had used in his writing, and other old files that represented uncomfortable family issues. This cabinet sat in the southeast, an area that represents growth and renewal. It seemed there was a correlation with the somber files and his current condition. He wasn't getting any new assignments and didn't feel supported by his family. He saw clearly that the old files were no longer useful and didn't need to be in his sanctuary. Clearing them out released him from the past and empowered him to move forward.

Fun in the office

In another home office I suggested to a woman who loved board games that she pull out her Hungry Hippo game she had had since childhood. She put it in the corner of her large desk so she could periodically play a few rounds in between writing law contracts. This was a perfect balance. Even though she had to take her work home, she still could have fun! The colorful game made her laugh and was close by to play with. She told me that a client called her at home and asked her what the noise was in the background. She laughed and told the man it was her therapy, the reason she was such an effective lawyer.

Reducing stress

Games and stress-reduction gadgets are popular, and there is a multitude of items you can buy to help you decompress. One Fortune 500 company has set up a juggling room for the employees to hang out, be silly, and move around in. Juggling is an activity that integrates the right and left side of the brain and body. Many other companies are realizing that laughter stimulates the endocrine glands and helps create overall well-being.

One stress-reducing system that has powerful exercises is called *The Healing Tao*. Mantak Chia, a Taoist master, teaches individuals and companies to relieve stress at the source, where it is stored in the body. The most basic of all the exercises he teaches is the Inner Smile. It stimulates the parasympathetic nervous system's "relaxation response," producing distinct physiological changes in your endocrine glands, nervous system, musculature, and circulatory system. In fact, nearly every system in the body can be dramatically affected by simply receiving a smile.

Make your home office fun and inviting— work doesn't have to be a grind!

The exercise requires that you know where your organs are located. The Taoists believe that if you send energy to the organs, you will keep them healthy. Mantak Chia relates all of the emotions with the organs.

Lungs	sadness, depression
Liver	moodiness, lack of motivation, anger, frustration
Heart	lack of vitality
Spleen, pancreas, stomach	anxiety and worry
Kidneys	fear

For example, when you are fearful, the adrenals send a shot of adrenaline, and the kidneys get stressed. Someone who holds all their emotions inside may be prone to stomach upset, ulcers, and headaches.

The Inner Smile exercise

This exercise requires you to sit quietly and close your eyes. Begin with the pituitary and pineal gland in the head. Lift the corners of your lips and send a smile to the organs. Smile down to the thymus, thyroid, and heart. Feel your heart open and take a deep breath, and let out a sigh. Feel love and happiness flow from the heart as you smile at it. As you smile at the lungs next, feel courage arise. As you smile at the spleen, stomach, pancreas, feel openness and fairness. As you smile at the liver and gall bladder, feel kindness. When you smile at your kidneys, feel gentleness.

Quick Tips

- Make your home office fun and inviting—work doesn't have to be a grind!
- Consider where clients need to walk to get to your office.
- Check your Nine Star Ki chart to help find colors that support you and your goals.
- Keep your work stress down with the Inner Smile and fun, stress-reducing gadgets.

Tai Chi, Chi Kung, and many more practices are great ways to circulate life-force energy through the body to keep you feeling young.

supportive **Kitchens,** *gathering* **Great Rooms,** *and* *lounging* **Living Rooms**

People can have very different purposes for kitchens and living areas. In some homes the kitchen is the central gathering place, while in others people relax in the living room. I knew a family who spent the majority of their time together in the kitchen. The kids would sit at the huge kitchen table and do their homework as the parents cooked dinner. The space was large enough, yet cozy enough to gather the family together.

Take some time to evaluate where you tend to gravitate to in your home. Look at why you think that is the case. Remember, color, compass directions, and furnishings all influence how you feel mentally, emotionally and physically.

Your intention and the room's purpose

Clarifying your intention for each room is the next step, and will assist you in finding what works best. Ask yourself what the room will be used for and what feeling you wish to cultivate in the space. Use the following chart for each room:

What is the main function of the room?

_____

Who will spend the most time in the room?

_____

What kind of atmosphere would serve this person best?

_____

What is your intention? To energize or to calm?

_____

Take some time to evaluate where you tend to gravitate to in your home.

Kitchens

Do you love your kitchen? Why? Is it because the sun streams in, rejuvenating you while you sip your coffee in the morning? Maybe it's filled with a lot of beautiful pottery and has a window you can watch the birds through as they feed at the birdfeeder. Is it the heated tile floor, or perhaps the floor-to-ceiling pantry? Beyond the physical, there is more than meets the eye. Look at your feelings and what you think about as you prepare food. Do you wind up thinking about work or all that you have to do? Perhaps you prefer to go out to eat because your kitchen is too small. What is the typical evening meal like? Noticing all this can help you have a clear idea of what purpose your kitchen serves and how well it supports your energy.

Many people feel a kitchen is the hub of family life and like it to be a social place, with places to sit close by the cook. Many houses have eat-in kitchens or a combined kitchen and dining area. A happy balance is the best answer. A kitchen isolated from the rest of the house can be inconvenient and too still.

Kitchens are special; they are where we prepare the food that nurtures us. Making the area where you cook convenient and comfortable will make your cooking that much more enjoyable. Having the stove in an open spot and where the cook has a view is preferable. Very often the stove faces a wall and has a microwave or cabinets above that stick out. Yes, this setup is useful, but not necessarily supportive to peaceful cooking.

One client of mine decided that a long alley kitchen was not only cramped but was no fun to cook in. Everyone had to pass through it to get to the room beyond. We investigated pulling out a wall and several other options that ended up not being possible. Finally, she decided to rip out the cabinets that were in the space above her head. She installed a six-foot-by-four-foot mirror that extended the full length of the counter and up to the ceiling. This added the appearance of double the space and drew in an abundance of natural lighting. Best of all, the entire mirror faced a window so when she was cooking she looked directly outside at the garden and the yard. Now when people enter the kitchen they think there is a whole room beyond the mirror and they can see her garden from in the kitchen doorway. And with the entry to the kitchen being perpendicular to the window, the mirror reflects a surround panoramic view.

The point is that the place where you cook your food should provide a nurturing experience. Some say the kitchen is the anchor in the house because of its nurturing aspect; but it is often overlooked in a new house plan. If you are building a home, pay special attention to the kitchen. Many of my clients who show me the floor plan of a home they are planning to build are focused on the kitchen area because they want it to have a certain feel about it. A mom with small children, for example, needs to see who's doing what. Families that entertain a lot usually have large, expansive kitchens.

Kitchens are special; they are where we prepare the food that nurtures us.

Check to see what elements are in your kitchen.

- Do you have linoleum, slate, tile, wood, or some other kind of flooring? Each has its own energetic feel. Plastic flooring is easy to maintain, but how does it feel?

- What materials are in other parts of the room—tile, slate, Formica, or steel? Notice all of the elements. I'm not saying one is better than another, but just observing the materials that are in your kitchen is important. Wood, for example, has a whole different feel than slate. A lot of wood can be overwhelming, especially if it's on the ceiling, walls, and floor. If you need a more grounded feel, slate, tile, and marble—each with its own unique feel—are all grounding. Just by bringing things into your consciousness, you will begin to have insights into what best supports your goals.

- See what's going on in your kitchen. Does it feel the way you want it to?

Take a compass reading and see which direction your kitchen faces.

You can notice this with cabinets and countertops as well. A client of mine just recently changed her countertops from Formica to granite— talk about a change! It completely altered the kitchen's energetics. She found that her family would gravitate to the kitchen, as if the granite had created a solid feeling the family had needed. (Not to mention that it added depth and beauty.)

Location of your kitchen

What part of the house is your kitchen in? Does it have an active feel or more of a settled feeling? Take a compass reading and see which direction your kitchen faces. You may gain insights into why family members are drawn to do homework at the kitchen table, or perhaps why they eat and run. Get a feel for whether or not it is a room that is conducive to talking out problems, or if it is a room that people rarely stay in. One family shared with me that family time is always spent around their kitchen table and it feels social and gathering. Noticing things like that can give you more understanding of how the rooms in your house can best serve you, as well as what area might be the best for putting on an addition.

North	fluid, adaptable, deep, activates the subconscious, dreams, and vision
Northeast	introspective, inner knowledge, transformative
East	active, upward-moving energy, new ideas
Southeast	philosophical, creative, disseminating
South	most active, expanding, full sun, illuminating, networking
Southwest	nurturing, supportive, calming, social, family
West	harvest, relaxing, tranquil, reflective
Northwest	direct, focused, responsible

Kitchens in the middle

A few years ago I was asked to speak at the Inns, Bed and Breakfast Association of Virginia. I was talking about optimum flow in establishments where many people share the same dining area and guests gather in a common area. A woman told a story about the bed and breakfast where she worked. She was frustrated that the kitchen sat directly in the middle of the building. All the guests gathered there and continually walked through, seeing it as a common space, which left her unable to focus her energy to get things done. The inn was not set up so that she could define the kitchen as a private area.

This was a paramount example of a highly activated space. The kitchen was not in a location where the cook could settle and organize. The guests were totally unaware and naturally gravitated to the center room. Kitchens are often a place where people like to gather. It works well when the kitchen is not en route to somewhere else, as in an alley kitchen or one in the middle of a home. Kitchens in the middle of a home can be too activating and chaotic.

Upward lighting can help balance out a dark or small kitchen by redirecting the energy upward.

Kitchens that are placed right as you enter a home can be convenient, but also can be hectic because they become the room that everyone goes into first. One woman had a kitchen like this, and she felt as if the children and dogs were always underfoot. She found that she was continually scooting everyone out so she could focus. The kitchen was in the southeast, which received the morning sun and felt supportive for morning baking. She needed to help settle down the energy and redirect the family in a different direction upon entering the home. She and her husband decided to build an extension with a greenhouse foyer, which provided a natural transition area that led into the living room. The same thing could be accomplished by using a screen or finding other ways to calm down the fast-moving energy. Just by giving it your attention and seeing the need to create balance, you will come up with ideas.

Lighting up your kitchen

Getting enough light in the kitchen is important.

Getting enough light in the kitchen is important. Most kitchens have down lighting, to shed light on the food preparation. Unless there is enough natural lighting, this may not be enough to balance out the cabinets and other fixtures, which tend to be on the top-heavy side unless there is space above the cabinets. Lighter-colored cabinets and the size of the kitchen can influence how noticeable this is. Upward lighting can help balance out a dark or small kitchen by redirecting the energy upward.

A client of mine in New York had a tiny little kitchen with very low ceilings and no windows, which can be the norm in a city. She took out the overhead cabinets and added one full-length pantry cabinet so as not to lose the storage space for dishes and food. This allowed her to mirror the full wall on the other side and actually pull in a view from far away in another room. It was amazing what transpired in her space. It felt roomy and as if she had a large window in her kitchen. The mirror was inexpensive, and the cabinet arrangement was a minimal expense as well. (If you decide to enlarge a space in your home with mirrors, ask the installers to use clips instead of glue. The glues are highly toxic.) She also discovered that the walls went up another foot above the suspended ceiling, so she removed it and added a beautiful ceiling higher up with supportive lighting. It was as if she had a different kitchen. Skylights can often bring light into a needed area as well. The colors you use, combined with the lighting, the location of the room in the house, and the materials (flooring, cabinets, countertops), can all affect how your kitchen feels. Depending on your intention, see what will help you reach your goal.

Living rooms to come together in

The living room is meant to be a place where we chill out and enjoy relaxing. Family rooms have taken on that role as well, especially for people who have a formal living room. Is your living room in a location that feels peaceful and relaxing? Is the room accessible and does it flow with the rest of the house? Do you gravitate to the living room to play cards, knit, or watch TV? Is your favorite chair there? Do you have colors in your living room that support your goals? Many people do not find that their living room feels useful or is a room they like to spend time in.

The living room is the one room that feels natural being near the front door. One couple had a living room that felt like a big hallway to the rest of the house. They couldn't find a desirable spot where they could put their furniture or sit and feel undisturbed. The room faced north and didn't get very much sunlight, which made it less desirable to be in. The wife wanted to add a room off the living room to give them a spot to relax in. The husband felt they could come up with some idea to resolve their problem without adding on.

After considering several options they decided to install a large bay window in the west-facing wall. The builder constructed the bay with the idea of cradling a couch within it. The extra three feet out from the wall added enough space to change the whole dynamic of the room. The couch became the focal point, and they put a few chairs near it with a table in between. The afternoon sun beamed in the window and created a new circulation pattern. It was a living room nook, near a fireplace, out of the central path. They painted the room a lively green and added sconce lighting to give an uplifting feeling. They followed the theme the next year and added bay windows in their den and kitchen.

The living room is meant to be a place where we chill out and enjoy relaxing.

If your living room feels small and you barely have room to move, consider working with ways to open it up energetically. Large mirrors on the wall opposite a window can add a new dimension to a room. If the room is long and thin, add the mirror on the narrow wall to expand the width of the room. A college graduate I knew moved into a tiny apartment in New York. She was used to a large home in the suburbs and felt totally squished in the small space. What she noticed the most was how irritable she felt. She was so uncomfortable that she stayed only a week and then she found an apartment twice the size.

Some people feel very uncomfortable in smaller places, and more often than not it is because their energy field is more expansive than the space. It is like being a hamster in a cage that is too small. Some people are naturally so expansive that they fill a space from across the room. This is not a measure of how big a person is; many small children fill a space with their energy. Children and teens naturally are filled with springtime energy that exudes all over the place. Many people living in too small a space find they leave home a lot, enjoying their time away from home. They are not conscious of feeling more at ease in larger spaces, but if the fact is brought to their attention, they will confirm that they do not feel their home supports their needs. For those feeling this way, the goal is to expand their space energetically or move to a location that feels expansive and comfortable. Our home is our sanctuary, and no one should have to avoid going home.

The goal is for you to feel that your living room is a place you want to go in, relax, and do the things you love to do. If you have a family room, that may take the place of the living room as your "chill out" room. Whether it's a living room or family room, create a nurturing place that invites you in to decompress.

Flooring throughout the house

Every object holds a vibration. Take a look around at every object and element that is in your space. Decide what supports you and makes you feel good. For example, do you have wood floors, or are they tile or

Some people are naturally so expansive that they fill a space from across the room.

slate? If you have carpet in one room and tile in another, stand in each room and see which feels more grounding and stabilizing. One is not necessarily better than another, but each has a feel, a quality that supports a goal. The goal may be to have the solid grounding that slate or marble brings. How does that differ from wood? Certain people do extremely well with wall-to-wall carpeting, but others only feel comfortable if they have hand-dyed or natural-fiber rugs. To some, this might seem obvious, but notice how you feel on a linoleum floor or in a mall or office with a synthetic floor surface—it is definitely different from natural flooring. Observe what each one feels like. Then take it one step farther—how does each one affect your energy level? Some say that the natural flooring can actually support the health of the occupants.

Remember that the goal is to create balance in your home, and that too much of one element can be overwhelming. A home with an overabundance of the tree (wood) element can feel overly active, supporting the occupants to be always on the go. A home with an overabundance of the fire element can support the occupants to feel scattered and have a hard time focusing. An overabundance of the metal element can support occupants to feel overly focused and worn out. An overabundance of the earth element can support the occupants to feel overly detailed, holding on, and stagnant. An example of an overabundance of the tree element is an all-wood building. Many people dream of owning a log cabin home tucked in the woods, surrounded by leaves and shade, the songs of birds, and the rustle of squirrels clattering over bark. In the last thirty years, it has become fashionable to remodel barns in such settings, and build houses that feature heavy, solid beams, or plenty of wood paneling.

In the past month, I have been asked to assist nearly a dozen people who are considering buying or who are already living in a log or wood home. The most important point to consider is the location of the home. Does the setting permit plenty of light to freely enter the house? Is it in an open field or is it surrounded by trees? How much natural sunlight actually enters the house. Check for extended rooflines, covered porches, or overhangs that might block sunlight. Lean toward homes that have plenty of large windows or skylights to fully illuminate rooms.

Remember that the goal is to create BALANCE *in your home, and that too much of one element can be overwhelming.*

If the interior of your home is all wood—wood walls, wood ceilings, wood floors, wood beams and posts—you may find that over time the preponderance of wood starts to bother you. Wood, unless it is stained a very light, almost white, color has a tendency to darken a room, so it is imperative to have plenty of ambient light.

As with all things, strive for balance. Wood can be charming, but balance it with light and color. Remember, when you go camping you aren't just sleeping under the trees; there are the stars, air, sky, and nature's myriad of colors.

As with all things, strive for BALANCE.

Chapter 12

Healthcare:

health and harmony

There is a hospital in Florida that has incredible Feng Shui. The main floor has water trickling through the middle of the building, and a multitude of plants and trees grace the entranceway. If you enter this building during the daylight hours, you are bathed in the natural light that pours in from the large windows and glass roof. Soft melodies can be heard in the background from a player piano. The glass elevators and the soft curves in the design, as well as the warm colors on the walls, all create a feeling of comfort and security.

The walkways meander around the water, giving you a feeling of peace and renewal. The patients cannot help but notice that the employees are smiling and helpful and seem to walk lightly, with a spring in their step. The joy of working in such a beautifully designed work environment spills over to the patients. This good feeling is contagious, and the patients also get caught up in it. One woman who worked there joked that people want to come in and get their gall bladder out! Use of lighting, color, and presentation all affect the energy levels and receptivity to health and well-being, as this hospital so beautifully illustrates.

Transformational waiting rooms

Few people look forward to going to see a doctor. Usually a trip to the doctor's office is necessary because of an illness or an injury. The patient is not feeling well to begin with and walks into a waiting room feeling that if he could be anywhere else, he would be. Waiting rooms often have stark, white walls with overhead fluorescent lighting and chairs lining the walls, filled with other people in various degrees of illness. Many health care practitioners have a glass wall separating the staff from the patients, often with a note taped on it directing the patient to sign in. There is no human contact, no warmth, no eye contact. The receptionist can open the glass partition when she wants to acknowledge the patient. Immediately upon walking into an arrangement such as this, the patient feels exposed and vulnerable and at the mercy of those individuals behind the glass wall. The impersonal setup can cause the patient to feel reluctant to share her concerns.

A nurturing and safe atmosphere

Any health care practitioner's office should create a feeling of comfort. It should be a safe place for patients to share their concerns. The reception area is the focal point, the first place the patient sees; therefore, it is imperative for this room to establish a sense of welcome. Warm colors such as soft shades of peach and yellow encourage patients and employees alike to relax and feel more at ease. The office employees will feel more energetic and upbeat and the office space will feel more grounded and less chaotic. Natural sunlight from windows allows the

The walkways meander around the water, giving you a feeling of peace and renewal.

most optimal lighting. Scattered table lamps and floor lamps soften the lighting around the room and enhance the feeling of comfort.

Live plants help support the doctor and staff as well as the patients they see. If conditions are not conducive to keeping plants alive and healthy, silk plants can be used in their place. Strategically placed pictures on the walls that reflect life and healthy living as a theme help lift the mood and energy of the office. The focus is on helping individuals create and maintain health.

Caring consultations

Having the patient sit next to the doctor, or with the doctor at a round table enhances the feeling of concern a doctor wants to convey. Nothing is more intimidating when you do not feel well than sitting on the other side of a large, expansive desk. There is no feeling of being connected to the person across the desk.

I have assisted many doctors and veterinarians with creating supportive office spaces. A local vet in Charlottesville, Virginia, created an office that has a wonderful feeling that instantly relaxes you. My pets don't have a hyper, "Oh no, I'm here again!" response when I'm sitting with them, waiting. He has installed fish tanks and warm tile floors in the reception area, which is much more comfortable than a clinical, sterile waiting room. He told me that he feels so much more centered and happy in his new space.

Dr. Bob's waiting room

One physician, "Dr. Bob," runs a successful cancer clinic. His waiting room used to have a variety of books and pamphlets around addressing health, cancer survival, death and dying, ways to deal with sickness, and other topics. All of the books conveyed sadness, despair, and hard work.

I asked him how he felt about his work. Dr. Bob said that he really enjoyed his work and had a deep concern for his patients and their well-being. He continued, though, by saying that dealing with the issue of cancer day in and day out made it difficult for him to find lighter things to bring balance into his life. He finally confessed that he did not feel that he

Warm colors such as soft shades of peach and yellow encourage patients and employees alike to relax and feel more at ease.

was helping the people who came in. "Everything is so clinical with all the tests and results," he said. I made a suggestion that he change the emphasis of the practice to that of "fun in the sun—dancing classes—all are welcome." He looked at me like I was crazy, and then he burst out laughing. At that moment, he got my message. Laughter heals and feels warm and fuzzy. Many of the great healers of the world are in sync with the Feng Shui principle of creating balance.

Creating a warm, friendly environment that incorporated the elements of light and fun was Dr. Bob's new mission. He closed his office for three weeks and began creating a new clinic better suited to meet his patients' needs, as well as his own. He had so much fun renewing his cancer clinic that at the end of the three weeks he felt like a new man!

Now when you enter Dr. Bob's office you see a large basket filled with small, wrapped presents. Each patient is asked to choose a gift, which they can open as they make themselves comfortable in the waiting room. Receiving a present always makes people feel warm all over. It is a way of connecting with their heart. His gifts are something small and silly and always provoke a smile, giggle, or an outright burst of laughter. What a wonderful way to enter a cancer clinic!

Laughter heals and feels warm and fuzzy.

He repainted the office a soft yellow. This shade of yellow is such a warm color that it immediately welcomes patients. He put up wall hangings of animals and children engaged in comical, spontaneous activities that strike you as funny as soon as you look at them. These pictures immediately bring a smile to everyone's face. One particular picture that seems to have a powerful, grounding effect on all who see it is from Sedona, Arizona. Dr. Bob brought this beautiful picture back from his visit to that special place known worldwide for its unique power to heal.

Dr. Bob replaced all of the generic, catalog furniture in his office with comfortable chairs. Each chair is covered with a bright, colorful print that reinforces the focus of fun and comfort. A large aquarium filled with lovely, colorful fish now graces this waiting room and contributes to the calm, serene feeling of the clinic.

The feedback from his patients has been overwhelming. Dr. Bob's patients began commenting that he appeared more relaxed and cheerful. He thought it was ironic that the patients were noticing his well-being, which had never happened before. Another change he noticed was that the patients in the waiting room were talking to one another as if they were at a social gathering. They created a support group for each other as they waited for their appointment. He discovered that after he removed the little glass doors between the office and the waiting area, the patients were less confused and solemn. They were able to take the focus off their illness and relax a bit. His relationship with his patients has changed drastically and to his surprise is now far less stressful. He enjoys going to work for the first time since medical school. All of this has affected his relationship with his family, his employees, his patients, and his friends.

Balancing nurturing with working

On a consultation with a clinic in southwest Florida, I found that although the people who had created the clinic shared the same intentions and goals, there seemed to be a great deal of turnover and inner-office conflict as time went on. Although the doctors and practitioners wanted to create a feeling of community and continuity, it seemed impossible. I discovered that the building was an **L** shape and lacked the southwest direction, which is the nurturing, supportive direction of a building. The building was energetically a more get-business-done-and-go-home kind of place.

We worked to incorporate a nurturing, more supportive energy that the patients would immediately feel. We opened up the flow in the floor plan and expanded the long hallways. The accountant had been complaining that it was difficult to work in the assigned space. I found it to be nonsupportive for keeping accounts, and for the financial/mental aspects of the business, but it was a perfect area for a reflexologist to practice peacefully; so the reflexologist moved into that space.

One change that immediately had a positive effect on the patients was the new entrance. Originally it had three doorways opening into a small entranceway. The multiple doors confused the patients as soon as they

We worked to incorporate a nurturing, more supportive energy that the patients would immediately feel.

walked up, and this created a feeling of uneasiness before they entered the waiting room. We eliminated two of the doors and widened the area to welcome the patients.

Trees covered over the actual entrance outside. Trees are wonderful, but if they close in an entrance and make it difficult to find, it will confuse the clients and make them feel uneasy upon entering. (The trees were also causing the building to rot.) A warmer entry path was needed from the parking lot to the building. The owners worked on the landscaping to give continuity to the walk from the parking lot to the entranceway. After the changes, a patient could be on remote control and easily make her way to the office. Now there is a single door to enter and a clear path leading to the main entrance.

The walls of the office were all painted warm colors to enhance the feeling of security and comfort. A lounge was created for the staff to talk and reconnect with one another. The employees all wanted the best for the clinic, and needed a place to voice their opinions and share their thoughts, and having a lounge made a huge difference. Each employee added to that space with pictures, flowers, funny sayings and other items. There was something there from everyone—it was truly a group effort.

Previously a formal conference room had been the only place for the staff to gather. Formal conference areas automatically put everyone on edge and do not support a relaxed, friendly atmosphere. We added a window and a mirror to the room, and replaced the long fluorescent lamps with sconce lighting. Now the conference room has a magnificent view that is enhanced by a mirror on the opposite wall. This room is alive and bright with natural light and energy, whereas before it was like a closed, dark closet with artificial light.

Staff members had reported that they felt they were not being heard and that important issues were not being addressed. This was causing many of them to leave and seek employment elsewhere. The employees who stayed had "invested" in the company in some way and they believed that working out the problems was a priority.

Many of the great healers of the world are in sync with the Feng Shui principle of creating balance.

I looked at each employee's Nine Star Ki numbers and we worked to focus their energies in the parts of the building that best supported each individual. The receptionist desk was moved to a central location in the front room. Behind the desk we placed a picture of children playing in the sun with trees in bloom. This colorful, lively picture that illustrated life and living replaced a picture of a leafless tree next to a dried up stream. The lack of life force in the original wall hanging was a psychological representation of a lack of renewal, not a health affirmation.

One fun activity I had the employees participate in involved using a very large roll of paper and having all the staff members draw a picture of themselves with their hands out. The first person drew his picture, then the next person added her picture, until everyone had a place in the picture and they were all holding hands! The howls of laughter alone brought an energetic change in the space. The employees continue to share stories about how their moods change upon entering the lounge.

We made other changes, but the continuity of the building was dramatically shifted—all at a low cost. A cleansing of orange and lemon spritz also helped, as did other intentional remedies. Patients have given the staff incredibly positive feedback, and the staff feels supported and energized.

The point I want to make here is that Feng Shui works on many different levels. Feng Shui supports our nervous systems, psychological states, and physical well-being. It also helps support the infrastructure of an office system, allowing everyone to thrive and see one another's strengths and weaknesses on a nonpersonal level.

Healing colors for patients and staff

I'm often asked to go to doctors' offices to help with design. In one such case the wife of a psychologist was helping with his office redesign project, and complained that her husband wanted to paint the whole place gray and dark maroon. She felt the colors were so down and depressing. The doctor felt that the color combination was basic and official, but he was open to other choices.

Feng Shui works on many different levels. Feng Shui supports our nervous systems, psychological states, and physical well-being.

Looking at the overall goal and plan for the center, I suggested a warm, soft yellow and sconce lighting throughout the building. Although the doctor did not like yellow, he liked the idea that the color would help his patients feel comfortable and social. I explained that yellow is a solar plexus color and it would support the clinic's goal to help patients open up and help get to the issues at hand. He could have chosen a variety of supportive colors, but yellow served multiple purposes in his case. Many of the employees had the metal element in their chart, and were feeling rushed and burned out. A gathering, centered feeling was needed to help bring balance to the space.

The building also had a playroom where patients' children could stay until the parent was finished with his or her appointment. A skylight was put in, which allowed sunlight to stream in, and a light green color was added to the walls with a stenciled ivy pattern. In his previous practice, where the walls were gray, the children often cried when their parents left them. The doctor noticed that after this room was painted, it ended up being a huge hit. The children hated to leave it.

In many areas of the waiting area and the employee room, they added a mural on the wall with a scene of people chatting together, which gave depth to the walls, expanding the space. Many patients commented that they loved coming to the office and that they felt well cared for. He noticed a huge change in the staff's energy levels and especially in how he felt.

Warmer colors help create BALANCE *to slow things down, and help people regroup and feel supported.*

Quick **Tips**

- Health and well-being of staff are directly related to the conditions they work in.

- Patients need comforting environments to feel relaxed and supported.

- Small changes can enhance a healing atmosphere.

- Color is a profound healing tool.

loving to **Shop** *and* *relaxing in* **Restaurants**

Applying the principles of Feng Shui is just as important in business situations as it is at home. Feng Shui supports not only you and your business, but also your clients and customers. The main goal of any service-related industry is to serve the needs of the customer in the best way possible. This goal or message must be conveyed as soon as a potential client contacts the business either by telephone or by physically walking through the door. We have always been told that first impressions make lasting impressions; at no time is this as critical as when a client first makes contact. The client can feel energetically whether or not the business is receptive to his or her needs.

The first employee a client encounters is going to set the tone for the entire business relationship. A bright, cheerful smile can not only be seen on the employee's face, but also heard in his or her voice. Soft eye contact can help the client feel more comfortable and at ease.

Hiring the right candidate for the job and creating a rapport with the employee is essential for the success of any business. It is important to create a work environment that supports the employees as well as the clients. This is where Feng Shui comes in. Shop or office arrangements, wall hangings, windows, lighting, and color or lack of color are just some of the elements taken into consideration when helping a business create a more harmonious environment.

There are many reasons that customers walk out of stores without making a purchase.

To buy or not to buy

You probably have been in a shop that was filled with a vast assortment of interesting items, but an uneasiness once you walked in the door kept you from really looking around. For some reason you felt uncomfortable, unable to relax and really browse. Shortly after entering, you wanted to leave. Perhaps there was an unsettled feeling in the air. Perhaps the employees were not eager to offer assistance. Perhaps you had the sense that the items on display had been there for a while, and they gave off a stale feeling. There are many reasons that customers walk out of stores without making a purchase. Often, if these customers were to be asked their reasons for wanting to leave, they could not articulate exactly why they felt the way they did. They just were uneasy, uncomfortable, and anxious to leave. All too often the reason has more to do with the Feng Shui of the business rather than the mood of the customer.

Ambiance

Stores that focus on making the customer feel welcome use a variety of techniques. They have employees who are very adept at creating attractive window displays that entice potential clients to enter. Inside, the displays are arranged to encourage the clients to browse, to carefully choose an item and inspect it closer. Some shops have a wonderful aroma thanks to a burning candle or flower arrangements placed around the shop. Music may be playing in the background. All of these creative touches are helpful in enhancing the overall mood the business is attempting to convey.

"Unseen" places

Just as important for the overall feeling of the business are the components that the clients do not see. Some business owners feel that because the offices and stockrooms are not part of the "public domain," they do not need to be anything special. The back office and employee areas are often just places to store things.

Just as a straight spine supports and maintains a person's health, the back-room area of a store or business literally supports a business. It is the space typically where the owner's office is, where the inventory is kept, and where the employees take their breaks and hold meetings. The back room may also be where special orders are taken, where deliveries are made, and where gifts are boxed and shipped. It does not matter how beautiful the floor and window displays are if the back rooms are small, uncomfortable, cluttered, and chaotic. Such conditions can cause the business to falter. Why? A sense of chaos and uneasiness will pervade the entire operation.

This may play out in different scenarios. More often than not, customers will enter, browse around a bit, and exit, not making a purchase. Employees may come across as frazzled and frantic, often unable to find an item that the computer shows to be in stock.

Back rooms are often stark white or a dingy color with fluorescent lighting. Typically these rooms are airless cubbyholes with no windows or natural light. Scenic posters and photographs, as well as warm colors painted on the wall can help to lighten the gloomy feeling and make the room appear larger. Small touches of color can do a great deal to help the employees feel supported and strengthened as they go about their jobs.

I was asked once to provide a perspective on a retail business that was doing well financially, but which the owners felt still had an uneasy air

Just as important for the overall feeling of the business are the components that the clients do not see. Back rooms are often stark white or a dingy color with fluorescent lighting.

about it that they could not quite put their finger on. The store had beautiful merchandise, but they were not really reaching the clientele they wanted to serve. The owners felt on edge, and therefore the employees could not relax.

A visit to the shop showed that the back room was a tiny space with no windows. It was packed from the floor to the ceiling with new merchandise and paperwork. In essence, the new items and the paperwork were bigger than the store space and the feeling was overwhelming. The area needed to be organized.

It was important to create a designated office area, preferably with a door that could be closed when necessary. I explained to the owners that the employees also needed a comfortable place, preferably with windows, where they could take a break and have the privacy needed to converse with the owners when customers were in the shop. This would help bolster their confidence and support them in being better able to serve their clientele. Once they installed shelving and repainted, and made a designated office area the atmosphere improved and so did their sales.

Happy shopping

The atmosphere of a shop is crucial for it to maximize its business. It is important to keep in mind that for many people the shopping experience at a special store is as much fun as the new item they take home.

In one evening lecture in Charlottesville, Virginia, I was discussing stores and businesses. A woman in the group, "Sue," posed a question about the hardware store she owned. Another woman, "Mary," immediately asked if this hardware store was the one she frequented in a particular shopping center. Sue acknowledged that it was, and Mary could not have been more effusive in her praise of the store. She enthusiastically shared her feelings about it. "It is so much fun to go into your shop. The wood floors give off the feeling that it is an old-time store. I can browse for hours and everyone is so helpful. I just love it!" What a positive affirmation this was for the owner of the store. Most hardware stores do not have the reputation of being "fun." This is a great example

The atmosphere of a shop is crucial for it to maximize its business.

of how the right personnel in the right setting can create a successful business scenario. The employees feel good about working for this establishment and their feelings of goodwill spill over to the customers.

Helpful relationships

A couple, whom I'll call the Sophies, phoned me in reference to some retail space in a nearby mall. They had an ongoing relationship with the owners of the mall, but it was rocky—sometimes up and sometimes down. The Sophies were afraid that they would be asked to leave their space in the mall because a large restaurant would be moving in and their shop space would be needed for the eating establishment. The owners of the mall had offered the Sophies a new space to move into. This was not a feasible option for the small shop owners because the proposed space was entirely too large and extremely expensive. They approached me with hopes that I could help them establish a more stable relationship with the owners of the mall. Their goal was to secure an optimum location within their financial means to replace their present space.

After touring the shop and getting the specifics of their business, I noticed that they had tiger and lion predator paintings in the northwest area of the shop that correlated with supportive, helpful relationships. This was in direct conflict with their goal of solid, sound interactions with others. I suggested that they replace the predator pictures with ones of people interacting in fun, social situations, such as a party. The pictures would reflect happiness and joy. We worked with mirrors to expand the space, and we addressed other issues they were having.

Several weeks after we had made the changes to the shop, Mr. Sophie called and told me that the mall owners wanted to help them find the perfect space for their shop. The space they suggested was in a prime location and was big enough for them to expand. Mr. Sophie went on to tell me that he felt there had been a shift in his relationship with the owners. He felt much more comfortable and at ease with them and with the choices they were presenting them. The Sophies have expanded their business, doubling their sales volume and their clientele. In the new location they incorporated fixtures that created optimum flow throughout

It is important to keep in mind that for many people the shopping experience at a special store is as much fun as the new item they take home.

the store, and added a sitting room area in the rear of the store with a fireplace in it. This helped to draw clients to the back, and made them feel more comfortable and at home.

Welcoming entryways

The position and location of a business entrance is extremely important. It dictates how much energy enters the building and this will reflect how much business occurs there. For example, the direction the entrance faces, how visible it is, the colors and message on the sign all have importance. Does it get natural sunlight, face the road, and have drawing power? Creating an entryway that can draw people in, create interest, and allow easy access is the goal.

Banks, for example, use large, formal entryways to create a secure atmosphere of a well-established business. Large office buildings and hotels also use large covered entryways for the same effect. They often have revolving doors, which create a vacuum effect and draw a sense of renewal into the building.

Easy entryways

A building with many entrances going into different businesses can cause confusion. People have to figure out where they need to go, leaving them confused and not as receptive to what is being offered. Department stores that sell many different items are challenged to communicate what they sell by the entryway and sign.

A furniture store contacted me for a consultation. This particular store was beautiful, with lovely furniture displays. The problem was the entryway. Upon opening the main door into the shop, customers were confronted by a wall that came to a point directly in front of them. In addition, two steps led to the main showroom entrance, and the customers had to look down as they came in. Confusing as well as hazardous, this entrance needed to be modified to help customers feel comfortable, not confused or wary, upon entering the store.

This same type of thing can happen in a large mall or office building. Many doors line up, and all of the businesses look the same from the

It's amazing to listen to people talk about restaurants, malls, or any business. They will always mention something about the building. "Oh, it's the cute building on the corner," or "They must do well—look at the building they are in." In other cases they may love the products in a shop, but say that it is too hard to get to or the parking is inconvenient.

outside. It is important to distinguish the doorway to your business to attract the clients. Putting small evergreens or potted flowers, painting a different color around the door, or attaching a sign to the door are all small changes that can help define your entrance and draw attention to your business. After all, isn't this your goal?

One gift shop I worked with had a post in front of it on the sidewalk. Potential customers were intent on getting around the pole and not pausing to look in. They would pass by, even though the shop had a lovely window display. The owners decided to use the post to advertise the business and draw attention to the shop. Winding little white twinkle lights around the post was all it took to create an entirely new feeling about the shop. Customers were then drawn in because they saw the post as a part of the store.

Delightful department stores

Department stores have the formidable task of creating displays along a path that draws the customer through the different departments without confusing them. Some department stores successfully encourage the shopper to stay and shop, using visual signs and ads to jar their memories of all things they may need in the store, or remind them of someone else they would like to buy a gift for. Color has a profound effect on the shopper's buying mood. Certain color combinations are powerful. Using three colors or more creates movement and interest. Having a clear intention of your purpose for a space is important.

Department stores are usually quite large and often have no windows. Because fluorescent lighting can be harsh on the eyes and nervous system, try using rose-tinted bulbs to bring natural warmth to a store (or your home!). Some large stores have mastered lighting and created a less generic feel that lends itself to shopping up a storm.

Using mirrors to open spaces

Drawing people into your store to view all of the merchandise is key to the success of any retailer. Shops in long narrow buildings must work extra-hard to lure shoppers to the back. Putting mirrors on the widest walls

Your establishment puts out a message to even those who have not physically been there. It's the "thought follows energy" theory: The thoughts that people form about your business are spread by people talking about it. Intuition as well attracts people to try a new business. The clearer your intention of what you want your business to say, the clearer people will feel it.

can help expand the feeling of the space. Creating balance is possible by arranging merchandise in a curved, winding path through the shop, which breaks up the straight-line feel of the room, and allows shoppers to meander to the back of the shop and around to the front again.

Restaurants

The entrance to a restaurant helps create the ambiance of the dining experience—it's the first impression. When the front door of a restaurant opens directly into the dining area, for example, the guests feel exposed and awkward. Diners who are already seated will turn to look at who has entered the room, causing the newly arrived to feel as if they are in the spotlight. It can be uncomfortable. It is best for a restaurant whose theme is relaxation and intimacy to have a separate area where the guests are greeted and comfortably led to their tables.

In contrast, think about what it's like to go into a fast-food restaurant. When you walk through the door, the layout leads you directly to the beginning of a (hopefully) fast-moving line. You wind through a serpentine roped area to the counter where you order, receive your food, and pay. The flow then directs you to a seating area with hard seats and small tables. The intention is to move you through quickly, to serve as many clients as possible in the shortest amount of time. The entrance will have a different focus: It needs to be highly visible and have easy access.

The intentions in these two scenarios are very different. Fine dining restaurants aim to create an atmosphere in which you will relax, order a glass of wine and have nice conversation, and perhaps linger after the main course for a specialty dessert and a latte. The fast-food restaurants, on the other hand, move you through as quickly as possible, maximizing the number of orders for their less expensive meals.

Dining ambiance

Creating a warm, inviting atmosphere that encourages diners to relax and enjoy the food and the people they are with will build the success of your restaurant. If possible, keep the seating arrangements out of the way of the general path of the dining patrons and wait staff. It can be

Because fluorescent lighting can be harsh on the eyes and nervous system, try using rose-tinted bulbs to bring natural warmth to a store.

uncomfortable and disturbing if the wait staff, with trays above their heads, pass directly behind diners who are trying to enjoy their food and conversation. (We have all had the feeling that the next tray would end up in our lap!)

It is best to have the tables in areas where the chairs or booths are privately tucked away or where the diner's back is not exposed to an active pathway. Subconsciously, it is most comfortable to sit away from the swinging kitchen doors. There is a great deal of activity in and out of the kitchen. Individuals who go out to eat are not interested in what is happening in the kitchen. Their goal is to enjoy the company and food.

Inviting colors and pictures for restaurants

Warm colors, cozy lighting, and expansive social paintings allow diners to relax and decompress.

- Oranges, reds, and pinks are great colors for restaurants. They stimulate passion, appetite, and social interaction. Gray, black, and dark blue may be cool. (It depends on the mood you want to create.)

- Upward lighting adds warmth to the walls. Candlelight also is warming and stimulates conversation. Rose-colored lightbulbs can bring natural warmth, while fluorescent lighting can be harsh on the eyes.

- Trompe l'oeil (illusionary art) of social events painted on the walls expands and opens the environment.

The mood you want to create

One client wanted to know why she attracted late-night party types to her restaurant. Although she loved the business, she felt it got too wild sometimes and was too much of a pickup spot. The walls were a deep, passionate red and the lighting was dim and gave off a hidden feel. On a subconscious level the bar said, "I can go in here to have a good time and forget myself until tomorrow." If the lighting had been brighter it would have conveyed a different feel. Either situation works, depending on what you are trying to achieve.

Whole Foods Markets (which started out as Bread and Circus health food stores) are very aesthetically pleasing. The minute you walk in the store you want to see everything they sell. They have everything under the sun: wood floors, warm lighting, fresh flowers, organic foods, vibrant colors, and the aroma of fresh coffee, along with a well-thought-out bakery and deli, fresh fish, salad bar, and a place to sit and eat. Any retailer's goal is to sell products, but Whole Foods Market has mastered creating an optimum flow and low-stress shopping.

Mirrors in restaurants

Mirrors can double a space, giving the illusion that the restaurant is larger and more active than it really is. Many establishments use mirrors behind the bar to create a psychological feel that they have more liquor than they actually do because the mirror image creates the illusion of many bottles.

Many restaurants utilize a mirror in the entranceway, which can reflect people in the waiting area as well as the cash register. The illusion created by the mirror invites people in and leads them to believe that it is a busy place—a "happening place." By creating this feeling, it entices more people to come in and see just what it is about this establishment that is attracting all of this activity.

Quick Tips

- Employee areas are as important as your storefront.
- Color can be used for motivation and support.
- Your workspace has a major impact on your well-being and creativity.

Mirrors can double a space, giving the illusion that the restaurant is larger and more active than it really is.

outstanding **Offices** *and creative* **Companies**

Enterprises large and small can use Feng Shui to augment their business, creating better employee rapport and cooperation, and ultimately more success. The tools covered earlier in the book can all be related to your office, building, and business. Use them to look at your business as a living entity. In other words, the building, the employees and the products are all interconnected. Creating balance between all aspects of your operation will bring greater harmony and help you have a little more fun every day!

Creating harmony

A computer company called me in for a consultation because they wanted to find out why their office felt so stressful. It was hard for the company to keep their workers. One particularly unhappy employee had such a negative air about her that you could feel her unhappiness just by walking by her office space. The main goal of the company was to decompress the negativity and to create a more cohesive and dynamic office force.

The office building was very long and narrow and had constricting, endless hallways. In this particular business, the manager's office was located at the back of a long, narrow room. It appeared that he was at the end of the corridor because of the moveable partitions that formed the cubicles for the employees' workspace. The energy in the room always ended up at his door.

Creating BALANCE *between all aspects of your operation will bring greater harmony and help you have a little more fun every day!*

The goal was to open up the space to allow more circulation. This would help dissipate the fast-moving energy that was channeled toward the manager's office. Warm colors were suggested to help create a nurturing environment. In the middle of the office, on a large wall, they installed a large floor-to-ceiling mirror to draw in natural light and reflect the trees and natural greenery from outside. Just adding this mirror gave the office a more energetic, uplifting, and enlivened feeling. The placement of the mirror helped break up the feeling of the long, narrow hall. Employees could position their desks facing the mirror, which gave them the opportunity to see out the window. The simple act of installing the mirror and removing the partitions helped the employees feel less stressed. It is amazing how light and nature help individuals feel more at ease and energized.

To help the individual worker who was so unhappy and felt that the office was taking advantage of her, I suggested that she reposition her desk. She had been working with her back to the opening of the cubicle. I explained how vulnerable and exposed people unconsciously feel with their desk facing the wall. Simply changing the position of her desk and allowing her to face out helped her feel more support and more positive about her working environment.

A successful interior design firm

A great example of how wall hangings can support workers, whether in a home office or in the home, comes from a consultation I had with a large interior design firm in Florida. The man who owned and directed this very successful firm managed many female employees. He contacted me with the intent of selling his firm. He was very frustrated and tired of handling the problems that surfaced with these employees, however minor they were. It is interesting to note that although he owned and managed the business, he had the smallest office in the building. It was the size of a bathroom and had no windows or wall hangings in it. He was a two-earth/two-earth, which influenced his care for his employees— he wanted them to have the optimum office locations. Even his wife had an office three times larger than his, with a lot of windows. Although the women were overwhelming him, he cared about how he could make their life easier. He came off as gruff to the employees, so they had no idea how he truly felt.

I suggested that he move out of this office space and into a larger, brighter office with more air circulation. He cited many reasons for not changing. He felt very strongly that his employees should have the space they needed to work and be creative. Because he did not want to change office spaces, we had to figure out what else would support him. I asked him what he loved the most. His reply was, "My grandson and my boat." I suggested he bring in the largest pictures of his grandson and his boat that he could find. The simple act of hanging these photographs on the wall helped him feel more in control.

Several weeks after our meeting, he called me to say that he was not going to sell the business after all. He had already painted the walls a supportive color, and his desk was situated such that his back was to the wall. The photographs helped pull it all together.

He understood that the reason his employees bothered him so much was because he wanted to make them all happy all the time. Just under-standing the dynamics of the situation helped him see it in a whole new light. A tiny change helped tremendously.

Simply changing the position of her desk and allowing her to face out helped her feel more support and more positive about her working environment.

Arranging for optimum teamwork

In another case, a glossy magazine firm contacted me for a consultation because they had expanded to the point where they had to separate the employees from the executives and wanted advice on where to put their top executives. This was extremely difficult because each executive had been working in close proximity to his or her particular group. The executives now occupied the floor below the employees. It was as if the balance had been disturbed. Our goal was to restore balance.

After being in tiny spaces with desks touching others, and having direct, eye-to-eye communication with his or her group, each executive now had a huge office to fill. Although the new situation might sound ideal, the executives were not comfortable with their new environs.

The new arrangement required the executives to interact with one another more often and outside of their usual conference-room scenario. Looking at their Nine Star Ki charts allowed for each person to be placed in the office space that best supported who they were and the role they played in the business. It also gave insights into how they could work together as a whole, valuing each for his or her natural abilities. It gave them a more objective, bird's-eye view of their interaction.

The building had fourteen-foot ceilings and wood floors, and in the middle of the executive floor there was a large open area—large enough to be a dance studio—giving the space a cavernous, vacant feeling. All of the offices had windows that looked out to the central area. My objective was to enliven this space, creating a nurturing centerpiece for the offices as well as a comfortable meeting place for the executives to come together to share ideas and resolve any issues at hand.

Plenty of light streamed through the windows, adding warmth and clarity to the space. They removed the fluorescent lighting and installed large light fixtures to give off soft, warm light for times when the sun didn't illuminate the room. Adding a rich, warm rug absorbed the echo and made the room more inviting. Large plants in terra-cotta pots combined grounding earth energy with the upward growth of the plants, bringing in a natural feeling of the outdoors.

Looking at their Nine Star Ki charts allowed for each person to be placed in the office space that best supported who they were and the role they played in the business.

One of the executives was inspired by the "Knights of the Round Table" theme and suggested a large, round table. Then they added soft-colored couches and chairs to circle the table. With these changes, the room shifted from a cavernous hall to a comfortable meeting place with continuity. It also balanced the mental emphasis of the "official" offices filled with papers, filing cabinets, and desks. This central room offered the executives the same opportunity—a place to plop down in a comfy chair and look out over the city and rest their minds.

Motivation

I got a call from a company in New York that was having trouble getting its employees motivated. The personnel director had a wonderful knack for hiring amazingly talented individuals with a great deal of vitality and enthusiasm. Ironically, once these individuals were hired, they seemed to lose their motivation.

The management could not figure out why the employees would sit at their chairs and look comatose. The setup had small cubicles in a part of the building that had a meditative feel to it. Someone could easily sit there and chant meditatively for a few hours, but it wasn't a spot to have one hundred employees trying to sell products over the phone.

The nature of the cubicle tends to limit the natural ability of the occupant to be productive. In most cubicle situations the employees' backs are exposed to people going by and their front is closed down, with a wall directly in front of them. People feel most empowered with their back against a wall, so they are not distracted and stimulated from behind. The front is then open to receive, to be creative and productive.

The result of sitting in a cubicle is that the worker finds it necessary to take numerous breaks to go to the rest room, get some more coffee, find something to eat, look for a co-worker to chat with—any excuse to get up and move around the office.

There happened to be no natural lighting in that part of the building, and the walls were blue. Last but not least, there were no paintings on the wall, or any other visual stimuli.

Large plants in terra-cotta pots combined grounding earth energy with the upward growth of the plants, bringing in a natural feeling of the outdoors.

Moving the employees to a more active part of the building was the first task. Allowing them to access their creativity and be at optimum productivity was the goal. They moved to an area that had windows and better air circulation. The cubicles were done away with, and floor lamps were brought in to direct the light upward. The lamps alone added an uplifting feeling. The part of the building they moved to had a soft green on the wall, which for the type of phone work being done there was a stimulating color that would support new and creative ideas.

An artist was hired to paint a wall mural of a scene looking out over the ocean—a vista that allowed the employees to see beyond themselves—creating an environment that supported the workers' natural abilities. On another wall a picture was added of people together enjoying each other's company. On a psychological level this added a feeling of group effort and one goal. The employees reported that the change made a big difference in how they viewed going to work. They had less eyestrain and were happy not to be walled off from the rest of the office. They felt more empowered and less distracted. The business found that their sales doubled, and seeing the employees so charged up was exciting. It was a win-win situation for the employer and the employees. Who could ask for anything more?

Desk placement

The owner of a travel agency was having problems keeping a receptionist. Every time she hired a new receptionist the person would become grumpy and feel ganged up on. Ultimately the receptionist felt unable to enjoy her job. I suggested that anyone who worked there would feel energetically inferior and the low guy on the pole because of the desk placement. We moved the receptionist's desk so that her back was supported by a wall and other employees were not directly behind her. She now had access to the clients coming in, and sat in a power position in the agency.

Allowing them to access their creativity and be at optimum productivity was the goal.

The owner reported that the receptionist perked up. She seemed to feel more supported by the move and didn't get distracted by activity behind her. She had full attention to give to the clients entering the office. Business picked up and overall employee harmony was achieved.

Business training: Conference rooms

Conferences and seminars are integral components of most business operations these days. Businesses of all types offer them as a way to communicate with their employees and with prospective clients. Employees are often encouraged to take seminars or attend conferences as part of their continuing education.

Often these meetings are held at a hotel or convention center, and the first thing everyone notices upon entering is the lack of energy in the room. Typically the meetings are held in rooms with no windows. To further perpetuate this feeling of being in a closet, the walls are often gray or blue, with a matching carpet. Some meeting rooms have a beige wall covering, which helps lighten the atmosphere. But often the overhead lighting is stark and obtrusive, and the walls are bare or have pictures with no intention behind them.

Unfortunately, a dark, lifeless room detracts from the importance of the message being conveyed. Even the speaker may not be operating at his best and may not be interested in what he is saying because he lacks energy! Warm lighting, circulating air, windows that open, plants, and comfortable chairs are all conducive to learning and absorbing new information. A relaxed and open environment helps the listener get the most out of the event being held in the room.

If meeting rooms were located away from the center of the building on the outer walls, they could have windows to allow in natural lighting and fresh air, which would be a big plus. Of course, the windows could be equipped with heavy "blackout" curtains that could be closed for audiovisual presentations.

The colors on the wall can have a profound effect. Shades of green, and wallpaper with openness and depth to the pattern can be uplifting.

Warm lighting, circulating air, windows that open, plants, and comfortable chairs are all conducive to learning and absorbing new information.

Depending on the objective, colorful soft shades on the walls help a room feel more alive. Finding the right color theme begins by examining the intention for the space. (Refer to Chapter 3 for more about color.) Interesting, intentional artwork that exudes an empowering feeling and most of all, the message of caring about how the participants feel in the environment will engage them. Eye-catching wall hangings that are lively and full of color can help improve the energy of any meeting room.

Table lamps and floor lamps scattered around the room help make it feel more comfortable. If you are a conference planner, imagine the setting as a place that enlivens all of your senses and in turn motivates your participants to fully engage in and enjoy the conference. If listeners feel uplifted by the surroundings, they will thrive. Many conference centers that use these ideas are booked years in advance because of the positive response they have received.

The bottom line is that people respond to their surroundings. Feng Shui can support you in making your business more harmonious and successful while empowering you and your employees. Take a look at your entire business and open yourself to trying something new. Have fun too.

Eye-catching wall hangings that are lively and full of color can help improve the energy of any meeting room.

flowers, plants, and
the great **Outdoors**

The landscaping around your home or office space can be enlivening and welcoming. Attractive greenery and walkways leading up to the building offer a wonderful feeling. The most striking landscaping I have ever seen combined water, flowers, plants, beautiful walkways, and trellises, which are appealing to the eye. No matter what you like, the most important factor is balance. For example, if you have square walkways, planting in circular patterns will balance the angular shapes. Considering the grounds from a holistic perspective will lead to what will best balance the area.

In Europe you often see tiered flowerbeds and small gardens tucked into small spaces, which create a quaint, cozy feeling. There are myriad ways to achieve the look you want. Look at your space to see what you have to work with. Read this chapter to get some ideas about what might work for your grounds, then let your intuition (and nature!) guide you in balancing your landscaping.

Plants and flowers

Garden flowers are so uplifting and look wonderful growing in a yard. Seeing renewal represented in growing and blooming plants subconsciously reminds us that there is life force bursting forth in all of us—a new beginning, bringing warmth to our lives and homes. Fresh cut flowers in our home or office help bring in a burst of sunshine. Flowers inspire writing, warm the heart, and are overall Feng Shui super-chargers.

While most offices are designed to evoke a strict business atmosphere, flowers and plants are often most appropriate, yet missing, ingredients from such spaces. Plants circulate the air and promote new growth, and the green color of stems and leaves stimulates our subconscious and motivates us. Every business needs a sense of growth and fresh ideas.

Plants such as bamboo, rubber plants, Boston fern, gerbera daisy, English ivy, dwarf date palm, peace lilies, lady palm, and areca palm help remove toxins and clear stale air. They are great for factories and high-rise buildings that have poor air circulation. Many closed shopping malls or large hotels incorporate plants, or running water such as fountains, because these elements evoke a sense of renewal. Shopping or staying in such spaces feels more supportive than in malls and hotels that are furnished with steel and inanimate objects.

Flowers

In Feng Shui, flowers are an easy and pleasant way to enliven any space. Each flower represents a certain energy and focus. The following list names the flowers and their qualities:

If you are feeling blue or down, go to a place that has beautiful flowers and plants growing, a garden perhaps, or a park full of wildflowers. Instantly, you will feel recharged.

Gladiolus gives a lifting feeling on many levels.

Daffodils The yellow/green combination is warm and uplifting, and is said to expand your business endeavors.

Gardenia stands for truth.

Daisy represents simplicity, wholeness.

Geranium promotes staying on your path.

Carnations take the focus off your problems and bring pleasure. They smell great and are long lasting.

Dahlias (perennial variety) are great for a flower garden. They are long bloomers, and have great upward- and outward-moving energy. Beautiful and elegant, they can recharge any space.

Roses and **holly bushes** are thorny. They can be a good barrier between neighboring yards where a distinction is wanted, but a general "look but don't get too close" may not be the message you want to give out. They are associated with style and finances. Roses placed in the western portion of a room are very favorable. Holly bushes in the front of a house are not as welcoming as a softer, free-flowing leaf bush or shrub.

Sunflowers provide a settled, calm feeling, as do other yellow blooms. Add these to dark rooms and offices.

Ferns These expansive, bright green shoots provide a fiery, energetic feel to a room and help fill empty space.

Chrysanthemums are said to be auspicious in the Chinese culture, where they are embroidered on pillows and clothing.

Hydrangeas are noted for a peaceful feeling, because of the shape and flowing feel.

Honeysuckle and **plantain lily** promote relaxation.

Lotus represents opening on all levels.

Keep in mind that all plants and bushes need space around them.

Plant shapes and the elements

Note the shape of a plant or tree and you will get a sense of what part of the yard to put it in. For example, if you want to introduce the fire element in an area to support it, try planting pointed leaf plants.

- Pointed shapes are of the fire element and are uplifting.
- Round shapes represent the metal element and are containing.
- Rectangle shapes represent the tree element and movement.
- Wavy, free-flowing shapes represent the water element and relaxation.
- Square shapes represent the earth element and are stabilizing.

Creating balance and following what brings you joy are best. Sensing how different plants and flowers make you feel will help you clarify what you want to create. Having fun outweighs any methodology. The key is knowing what you want and using your intention to achieve it. Feng Shui is all about observing nature, its cycles and its wisdom.

Plants for health

To promote health, look for dark, rich, green leaves and solid stems that stand well on their own. Long hanging plants can drag down the energy in a room; keep all spider plants strictly manicured or they will take over. Jade plants are very favorable because of their depth and sense of longevity.

Many people send flowers to the hospital when a friend is sick or when a baby is born, and of course flowers are important at weddings and special events. Symbolically, these gifts of flowers speak of the sense of renewal or new life ahead. Our daily lives, however, can also do with a boost of energy. Add fresh flowers to your home every week. It helps keep the overall Feng Shui charged and circulates energy in your home.

Plants are also a good Feng Shui cure for sharp corners or large empty spaces. Many Feng Shui adjustments are made to make one feel more aligned with nature and natural rhythms; before you try suggestions that may seem odd to you, such as a mirror here, or a crystal there, try using

Creating balance and following what brings you joy are best. Sensing how different plants and flowers make you feel will help you clarify what you want to create. Having fun outweighs any methodology.

a plant first. That may be all you need. Silk plants can add the needed color and expansive feeling you want to a room without creating more work for yourself. It depends on the plant or flower you choose.

Pots and patios

Outdoor pots and planters serve two purposes. First, they define the area where you put them in an entryway, stairway, or porch. They give balance to the stairway or porch by adding upward-growing, vertical energy to the horizontal surface. Second, a container creates depth and a solid feeling to a surface. Verticals define the horizontal shapes on the ground plane, but also affect the quality of space they contain. This is why enclosed patios feel like a defined room. Playing around with this concept allows you to transform areas in your yard that just aren't the way you want them to be.

Pathways

Edging on pathways can create the most enchanting areas in your yard, whether they meander around your plantings or lead you to your destination. Bricks set on end are a lovely way to define a border in a garden area. Bricks laid on either side of a stone or other kind of path will make it look like it is all one walkway, yet create a different pattern. Decks and porches can be done this way as well, using different wood and stone arrangements. Many oriental gardens look elegant because of their decorative patterns in the paths and decking. They use shapes like triangles, circles, and curves to create ambiance and a peaceful feeling. Each piece of wood or stone is laid to create an overall effect. There is a purpose to everything that is created—hence the name Zen garden.

Flowing driveways

Circular driveways create a feeling of continual flow, and are nice from a practical point of view because you don't have to back in and out. One man told me he installed a circular driveway so he wouldn't have to strain his lower back and neck when backing out of the driveway and to give himself the feeling he was always going in the right direction. Circular drives are stately because they create balance in proportion to a

Adding birdhouses can enliven stagnant areas.

Quick Tips

- Planting flowers and flowering trees in your yard can make you feel terrific every time you return home.

- Terra-cotta pots that define entryways and patios add energy and color.

- Trellis-type garden fixtures with flowers that can grow up and out help balance areas that need to define a boundary.

- Circular and free-flowing gardens can outline a pond or define areas of a yard.

building. Many huge mansions create the illusion that they are even grander than they are because the driveway is an extension of the entryway. Some large hotels establish themselves by their grand entryways as well. (For more information on entryways see Chapter 8.)

A cute cottage

A client of mine had a cute cottage that she loved but felt that perhaps it was too small for her. The main problem I saw was that this tiny cottage was surrounded by shrubs suitable for a mansion. Huge boxwoods covered the sides and back of the home. She had major mildew problems and virtually no sunlight entered the home. The shrubs hugged the building and covered the roof in some spots. The house could not breathe. Her symptoms correlated directly with what was going on with the house. She had been feeling overwhelmed with trying to keep up with all that she needed to get done. In some of her close relationships she felt unable to have enough breathing room and time for herself. I suggested a few things for the inside of the home, but the main emphasis was on the shrubs. The shrubs needed to have more space to thrive and the house needed to breathe.

Moving shrubs can sometimes kill them, so figuring out how much she could cut them back was the question. Finding a new spot for them and adding new, more proportionate plantings around the home would be the best. This would alleviate the mildew problem and bring the much-missed sunlight back into the house.

Clear running fountains

A mail-order entrepreneur who sold financial information by mail called me because for six months his business had not been as profitable as in previous years. His home, grounds, and basic overall Feng Shui were fantastic and really supported his goals and family as a whole. It was a mystery why his income had dropped until he happened to mention as we walked towards a fountain that it was not functioning as well as it could be. His wife piped up and said they had lost their gardener six months earlier—he had maintained the grounds, keeping the fountain

Trees and shrubs create borders and boundaries between neighbors.

free of leaves and scum, and functioning happily. All of our eyes opened wide. The gardener was called immediately, and shortly after, things were back up and running—literally!

Trees that define

Trees and shrubs that create borders and boundaries between neighbors help define a yard with a softer feeling than perhaps a fence, although fences with plants growing up them can look beautiful. Defining your yard is helpful. I've seen many disputes over neighbors infringing on each other's space because the boundaries are not clearly defined.

Trees such as boxwoods, pines, bamboo, and junipers stay green all year and give a sense of stability, longevity, and stamina in a yard. Keep in mind that trees growing too close to the home or driveway can be overwhelming, not to mention that the root systems can suffer.

Walk around your property

Small changes can have a profound effect. Take a walk around your property and look for dead limbs, piles of brush, or old things that no longer serve you. Let your intuition guide you as to what needs attention. Even small things can affect you on a subconscious level. Broken fences, empty cans, an unorganized garage and unidentifiable piles of stuff can be overwhelming when they add up.

Nature is an integral part of our existence. It surrounds us, brings us joy, and is our reflection and teacher. Nature transcends cultural beliefs and joins us all together. The Five Elements, Compass Directions, Nine Star Ki and Feng Shui are all based on the rhythms of nature. Feeling these cycles and reflecting that awareness in all that you do will bring more harmony and balance into your life.

Fruit trees are not easy to grow but can be fun, and often the fruit can be eaten and used for cooking.

Oak represents endurance, hence the name "mighty oak."

Nine Star Ki

The history of Nine Star Ki

Nine Star Ki is based on an ancient Chinese text called the *I Ching*, (pronounced *e king*) the *Book of Changes*. All of life is based on the principle of change. In fact, it is often said that the only constant in life is change! The *I Ching* is perhaps the oldest book that comes to us from the ancient Taoist philosophers. Conceptualized by Fu His (2953–2838 B.C.), the first emperor of China, the *I Ching* is considered a guidebook for a balanced life.

I Ching astrology, or Nine Star Ki, is the understanding that cycles repeat every year, month, day—down to minutes and seconds in the natural world. These cycles are observable and have a pattern to them. The pattern is best represented by the eight trigrams/numbers of the *I Ching*. The center makes up the ninth element, which results in Nine Star Ki. Each of the trigrams/numbers represents a quality and direction of energy.

The *I Ching* explains that in winter the energy of life is stored deep in the ground, and therefore it is a time for introspection, reflection, and regeneration. Spring is the time for new beginnings and planting seeds for growth. That's why spring cleaning allows new things to enter our lives.

It is often said that the only constant in life is change!

Nine Star Ki and you

We all came to this life with different elemental energies depending on our time of birth, season, and year. Nine Star Ki explains these differences and is a guide to understanding yourself and others, as well as our interaction with the world.

Three numbers represent these energies in your Nine Star Ki chart. In this book we will look at the first two. Your first number represents your true essence, or essential nature (your constitutional nature). The second number represents your emotional nature. The third represents how you appear to others. Understanding the relationship between your essential nature and your emotional nature is my focus in this book.

The personality types

Your chart includes a combination of two or three elements. So, when you use the charts that follow to figure out your Nine Star Ki chart, you might find, for example, that you are a two-earth for your first (constitutional) number/element and a nine-fire for your second (emotional) number/element. Your numbers are then (2,9). These combinations are described in the Nine Star Ki personality descriptions.

How to find your numbers

If you are born between January 1st and February 4th take the year before. For example, if your birthday is January 28, 1988, take 1987 as your birth year.

Use the chart on page 143 or use the following manual method to determine your first Nine Star Ki number. First take the year of your birth and add all the numbers together. For example, say you were born in 1951. You would add 1, 9, 5, and 1 together to equal 16. You need a number less than 11, so add 1 and 6 to equal 7. Now take 7 away from 11, which equals 4. Your first Nine Star Ki number based on the year of your birth is 4.

Here is another example. If you were born in 1959, add the 1, 9, 5, and the 9 together, which equals 24. Since the total, 24, is greater than 11, add the 2 and the 4 together to bring the total to 6. Subtract this number from 11, as you did in the previous example, and the result is 5. For someone born in 1959, their Nine Star Ki number is 5.

Use the chart below to find your first number

9	Fire	1901	1910	1919	1928	1937	1946	1955	1964	1973	1982	1991	2000
8	Earth	1902	1911	1920	1929	1938	1947	1956	1965	1974	1983	1992	2001
7	Metal	1903	1912	1921	1930	1939	1948	1957	1966	1975	1984	1993	2002
6	Metal	1904	1913	1922	1931	1940	1949	1958	1967	1976	1985	1994	2003
5	Earth	1905	1914	1923	1932	1941	1950	1959	1968	1977	1986	1995	2004
4	Tree	1906	1915	1924	1933	1942	1951	1960	1969	1978	1987	1996	2005
3	Tree	1907	1916	1925	1934	1943	1952	1961	1970	1979	1988	1997	2006
2	Earth	1908	1917	1926	1935	1944	1953	1962	1971	1980	1989	1998	2007
1	Water	1909	1918	1927	1936	1945	1954	1963	1972	1981	1990	1999	2008

There is one important point to be aware of in this ancient Chinese system. The Chinese New Year begins on February 4. If you were born between January 1 and February 4 of any given year, you would calculate your Nine Star Ki birth year as the previous year.

For example, if you were born January 13, 1962, you would consider your Nine Star Ki year of birth as 1961. Add the 1, 9, 6, and 1 together, which equals 17; add 1 and 7, this equals 8. Then subtract 8 from 11, which equals 3. In this example, the Nine Star Ki number would be 3.

Finding your second number

Now you know how to work out your first constitutional Nine Star Ki number. There is a second number that represents your emotional nature.

To discover your second number, please look at the following chart. As an example, if you were born March 7 and your first Nine Star Ki number is a four-tree, you will look in the first column where the 1, 4, or 7 are located and follow it down to where it meets March 7. That shows you that your second, emotional number is seven-metal.

Finding your second number

| Find your date of birth | If your <u>first</u> Nine Star Ki Number is: | | |
	1, 4, or 7	5, 2, or 8	3, 6, or 9
	Then your <u>second</u> (emotional) number/element is:		
February 4 to March 5	**8** earth	**2** earth	**5** earth
March 6 to April 5	**7** metal	**1** water	**4** tree
April 6 to May 5	**6** metal	**9** fire	**3** tree
May 6 to June 5	**5** earth	**8** earth	**2** earth
June 6 to July 7	**4** tree	**7** metal	**1** water
July 8 to August 7	**3** tree	**6** metal	**9** fire
August 8 to September 7	**2** earth	**5** earth	**8** earth
September 8 to October 8	**1** water	**4** tree	**7** metal
October 9 to November 7	**9** fire	**3** tree	**6** metal

If your main Nine Star Ki Number is 1, 4, or 7 follow first column down.

If your main Nine Star Ki Number is 5, 2, or 8 follow second column down.

If your main Nine Star Ki Number is 3, 6, or 9 follow third column down.

Understanding the relationship between your constitutional nature and your more inward emotional nature is very important. An editor I know says that as a young adult she would write beautiful stories and create works of art with inventive inspired information and then she'd edit it to the point that there was no story or article left. She has a three-tree constitutional number and a seven-metal emotional nature. The three-tree side is inventive, loves to put her ideas down on paper. The seven-metal side wants to curtail any unnecessary information, bringing it into a finished, well-written piece. Unfortunately, even though the two sides are useful, the seven-metal side tends to cut down or override the three-tree side and not allow her free-flowing expression. Her realization when discovering her tendency was that it was best to allow someone else to edit her work so that she could honor her free-flowing writing style. She saw how both these sides of herself needed to be honored.

Business applications of Nine Star Ki

It is possible to utilize Nine Star Ki in business to maximize the workings of a team in any given situation. Nine Star Ki helps everyone involved to understand the cycles that make up their everyday life and to move in harmony with the natural order of the universe.

In an imaginary office setting it is possible to see how each of the Nine Star Ki personalities may react on a team project. This is a valuable tool for any manager to utilize the team members to the best of their abilities. When individuals are recognized for their strengths, they are better able to support the team as a whole. Recognizing the innate ability in each person also validates them and helps them to continually grow and develop in their own special way.

Understanding the relationship between your constitutional nature and your more inward emotional nature is very important.

Together all the Nine Star Ki personalities each bring their own unique set of talents to support each other to achieve the common goal. When each team member is recognized for the strengths he or she brings to a project, the project will be successful, as will each individual working as a team member.

One-water individuals are inventive, have vision, and are insightful. They can look at all the angles of a situation. Having a sense of clarity allows them to move forward towards any goal.

Two-earth individuals use their fine attention to detail to discover all the facts. Their emphasis is on obtaining a harmonious outcome for all working on any particular project. The tendency of two-earth individuals is to consider all that is involved.

Three-tree individuals want to get all the facts out in the open efficiently and get quickly to the point. Their high energy level keeps any project alive and moving. When they are able to incorporate the ideas of others and be flexible, their vitality and enthusiasm are unmatched.

Four-tree individuals add a philosophical approach. Their sense of adventure puts them on a continuing quest to broaden their skills. They bring worldliness to the project and their input is well rounded.

Five-earth individuals are solid and confident and gravitate towards the center of any project they are involved in. They are usually terrific at adding the necessary information to bring about success. Five-earth individuals trust others to do their part as the key to the overall harmony of any project.

Six-metal individuals add the endurance and focus of getting things done. They need to rely on others to do the nitty-gritty work. When all the information is gathered, they are the ones to take the ball and run with it. They make great team leaders and should always follow their first gut feeling in any situation.

Seven-metal individuals are also highly focused. They usually focus their attention on learning how things go together and figuring out the mechanics of the project. They have a great gift for making complex things seem simple. They make great managers, using their highly intuitive nature to bring insight and higher knowledge to any project.

Eight-earth individuals have a tendency to keep to themselves, yet they provide a solid ground for others to stand on. If a crisis should erupt and everyone is panicking, it will be the eight-earth individual who maintains his or her inner harmony.

Nine-fire individuals enjoy being the center of any team and excel in a leadership position. These individuals are excellent at making and developing contacts in any community or organization, and therefore are good at public relations. They add their warmth and sense of humor to any project.

Together all the Nine Star Ki personalities each bring their own unique set of talents to support each other to achieve the common goal. When each team member is recognized for the strengths he or she brings to a project, the project will be successful, as will each individual working as a team member.

Nine Star Ki is a lifelong study. Observe these new ideas in your daily interactions with others. At the heart of these teachings is the core concept that we are all connected, and each of us has unique gifts that we can use to contribute toward a better world. The way each of us expresses our own truth is only part of the picture. We are all different expressions of the one whole, many colors of the perfect rainbow.

Nine Star Ki is a lifelong study.

1-Water *the visionary*

Water individuals are the visionaries. They have an amazing ability to see the big picture. Their ideas are ahead of their time and they are often considered pioneers in their field. My sister-in-law is a great example of this trait, as she was one of the first women bush pilots in Alaska. There is nothing like a good adventure for one-water people.

They are usually deep thinkers and possess a great deal of endurance and inner strength. Inventors and songwriters often have water in their charts, as do healers. Healers use the healing current that flows through their hands. Inventors and songwriters are the same—the ideas for inventions and songs flow through their minds and hands to paper. These types of professions help keep the one-water personality in the flow with their creativity. Writing, drawing, painting, and dance are also examples of free-flowing outlets that help keep a one-water in balance.

If a one-water is unable to express their creativity, whether it be in their work or in their personal life, they might feel unhappy and lose their enthusiasm. They need to be able to express their vivid, futuristic, and mysterious selves through free-flowing activities. Low back pain and reproductive problems may surface when one-waters are not in touch with their emotional and creative needs.

I know a one-water man who was in the Peace Corps in South Africa during the eighties. He knew that supplies were limited, so he would collect anything he could find that could be useful. He had the foresight to see how nails, paper clips, pieces of wire, string, and other odds and ends could be used for inventive purposes. He made a wire pull that kept clothes off the ground to keep the scorpions from crawling inside. All of his Peace Corps buddies humored him but thought he was crazy. A few months down the line, when supplies were gone, they all came to him to ask if he still had any wire or a nail that they could use.

Writing, drawing, painting, and dance are also examples of free-flowing outlets that help keep a one-water individual in balance.

When one thinks of water in nature, it is easy to see water flowing over rocks and dirt, or gently lapping upon the sandy shore of a beach. Movement is as important for those with water in their charts as it is in nature. When water ceases to move, stagnation occurs. Think of a pond with no movement. They need to keep their energy alive and flowing and enjoy friends, laugh, and have fun.

Water individuals have been known to stay in a nonproductive situation for longer than may serve them due to their adaptable nature. They have the ability to see a person's potential and therefore what the future could hold. Water individuals usually have the ability to go with the flow, but if they feel strongly about something they can become fixated on the point, and be very persistent. These individuals feel most in balance when they are following their dreams and keeping the adventure alive.

Trigram **Water**

Their trigram in the *I Ching* is water, which means they have the qualities of all bodies of water like streams, ponds, lakes, bogs, or oceans. Water is enduring. It adapts easily to the situation it is presented with.

One-water children

When I think of one-water children, I imagine them sitting at the window with a wide-eyed look, wondering what the world has to offer next. True inventors and visionaries, their minds are inquisitive and intuitive. Nature can provide a wonderful support system for these children—going for nature walks, hunting for crabs in hidden pools down on the ocean edge, any quest for adventure. They possess a tremendous amount of inner strength and endurance that is common to all water personalities.

One-water children are also extremely creative and adaptable, and are constantly thinking about what they want for the future. My nephew who is eight years old is hooked on a computer game where you have to build and manage an amusement park. It takes a keen mind to consider all the future events, such as how much money to charge for rides.

One-water children are also extremely creative and adaptable, and are constantly thinking about what they want for the future.

It is not to say other children would not love the game, but it is as if he is using the skills to go beyond the boundaries of the amusement park. Typically one-water children are whizzes at the computer. One of my clients has a son who has known his way around the computer since he was four! He has astounded teachers and computer instructors more than once to cause them to exclaim, "He is going to be the next Bill Gates!"

It is important for parents of one-water children to encourage their vision. One-water individuals have a broad, expansive view of the world. Encouraging them to explore their natural curiosity and enrolling them in classes that they express interest in are ways to support these children.

One-water children express themselves differently in the world depending on the second (emotional) number. If nine-fire is the second number, the child will most likely be more fiery and possibly have emotional outbursts now and then.

It is important for parents of one-water children to encourage their vision.

Relationships with other people

One-water individuals blend best with six- and seven-metal, who support them. One-water individuals combine well with three- and four-tree individuals. One-waters tend to have a more difficult time with nine-fire individuals; two-, five-, and eight-earth may make them lose their focus. This does not mean that one-water individuals cannot have relationships with two-, five-, and eight-earth or nine-fire individuals, it simply means that they must work on the relationships a bit harder.

Combinations for one-water individuals

Water/Tree

This is a good, supportive combination, just as in nature, water supports the growth of the trees. These people have the ability to act on their dreams but it's important for them to keep a positive outlook because they have the tendency to worry. These individuals have tremendous imagination and vision, and are usually very knowledgeable.

Water/Earth

The earth side may create boundaries for the free-flowing one-water side of themselves. It is the same situation in nature; the earth creates the banks or shore for the water to be contained. While it is always good to have boundaries, their responsible earth nature may hold back the water/earth individual from doing things they would like to do. The grounded, strong earth nature just has to leave leeway for the free-flowing, inventive, creative water side. It is important for the water/earth person to honor both sides, to follow their dreams. Remember, the one-water person is the bush pilot going out on a limb, keeping the adventure alive in whatever he or she loves.

Water/Metal

Six- or seven-metal combined with one-water is a supportive combination. Metal and water are supportive of each other in nature, and that is how it manifests in relationships also. One-water individuals with either of the metal numbers as a second number have a solid, well-rounded way about them. They can become quite serious, so it is important for these individuals to have fun and enjoy themselves.

Water/Fire

Think of the properties in nature: Water can be used to put out fire, yet it can exacerbate a grease fire. The fire side of this combination must fight hard to shine. The one-water can encourage the nine-fire side to go deeper. The tree element helps to bridge these opposite sides, so activities such as walking and hiking in a beautiful place will bring this combination into balance. It usually is rejuvenating for one-water/nine-fire people to get outside in nature—it helps them manifest new ideas. It is helpful for these people to honor both sides of themselves. Getting out in the limelight in some way and getting recognition for their talents would be helpful. The fire side may wilt away if unable to be true to its expressive, entertaining side. Having a higher purpose in life also helps stabilize these individuals.

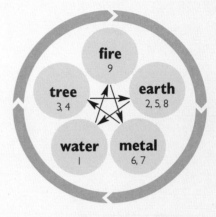

Nine Personalities

Water/Water

People who are water/water combinations are often determined and strong-willed because of the intensity of the water element. Like the other double same-number combinations, they are usually on a mission. They need to stay grounded. They definitely have the ability to go where no one has gone before—true visionaries.

Famous one-water individuals

Jim Henson, the creator of the Muppets, had an unrivaled imagination. Both of his first elements were water (1,1), extremely creative. Each character he created had the ability to depict all of our favorite moods and idiosyncrasies. He gave us permission to embrace the emotions that we often label as silly and childish. We are able to laugh at ourselves as we laugh at his characters presenting the emotional qualities we see mirrored in our own lives.

Charles Darwin was a (1,8). Darwin was a visionary who had an amazing futuristic approach. His eight-earth side would emphasize his practical, pragmatic, systematic side.

Errol Flynn (1,4) and Louis Armstrong (1,4) were two entertainers who were ahead of their time and legends in their own right. Carly Simon (1,4), Eric Clapton (1,7), Van Morrison (1,2), and Benny Goodman (1,5), all recognized for their musical ability, are all water individuals. Van Morrison (1,2) writes songs that are timeless (one-water) and often have to do with people in life and relationships (the two-earth nature).

Steve Martin (1,2) and Henry Winkler ("the Fonz") (1,9) also have water in their charts. Both of these extremely talented actors can truly "go with the flow" and become the character they are cast as. Henry Winkler can portray a 1950s greaser with a leather jacket and a motor-cycle as easily as he can portray a character in a Shakespearean play. His nine-fire emotional number allows him to be very expressive and his one-water side is cool and subdued. Steve Martin tickles your funny bone because he is able to depict so many personality types (two-earth) and he definitely is ahead of his time (one-water).

Some of my favorite one-water women are Goldie Hawn, Bette Midler, and Diane Keaton.

Ron Howard, now a famous director who is well known for his tremendously successful movies such as *Apollo 13* and *Backdraft,* grew up on television. He is remembered for his heartwarming portrayal of Opie on *The Andy Griffith Show* and as a teenager in the television show *Happy Days.* Howard is now well known as a visionary in the movie world, someone who is adept at using his knowledge and foresight and turning it into successful movies.

Some of my favorite one-water women are Goldie Hawn, Bette Midler, and Diane Keaton. These three actresses were all in the movie *The First Wives Club,* making a strong statement for women to stand up for what is best for them. Goldie Hawn and Bette Midler share the same second number eight-earth. Diane Keaton has a seven-metal second number. All three of these women have stamina and have played important roles in movies that have made a statement for a cause.

J.R.R. Tolkien authored *The Hobbit* novels. These timeless books are still popular today. Madeline L'Engle (1,8) is another author who has presented her audience with priceless spiritual works that are timeless and have inspired and supported young and old alike for decades.

Steve Martin tickles your funny bone because he is able to depict so many personality types.

2-Earth *the friend*

Two-earth individuals care a great deal about the relationships in their lives. Most of the time they are receptive to others and are very nurturing. If pushed to depleting their nurturing nature though, they can become fed up and you will hear about it! Most two-earth people enjoy being in relationships. Whether it is with family or friends, they delve into all aspects of life through relationships.

People love to tell two-earth individuals their intimate life stories. A two-earth woman I know is a secretary in a busy doctor's office. Every patient that comes in gets her full attention. They know that she really cares about them, and as a result, they tell her things they would not tell their best friend! Her sincerity is really apparent. She is truly interested in what the other person has to say. Many two-earth men are either a girl's best friend because they are wonderful listeners, or they are the rugged Navy SEAL type.

Most two-earth people are detail oriented. All of the individuals with earth numbers in their charts hold a warehouse full of information. One way this may show itself is if you ask a two-, five-, or eight-earth what restaurant to go to. You would hear every detail about how to get to the restaurant, what the specials are, and what server to ask for! They can save people time doing the research. Of course, this quality can manifest in other ways. I have a client who has files of handouts she has collected over the years. She has saved these files just to give information to her friends and business associates who ask for it!

Sometimes earth individuals can get stuck in the details. Being natural collectors, they often feel they need just one more piece of information and then they will be able to move forward. Clutter can be an issue with some earth people. Deciphering what is clutter and what to keep is important; once that has happened, the individual feels lighter and more energized.

People love to tell two-earth individuals their intimate life stories.

It is quite common for two-earth individuals to put the needs of others before their own needs because of their gracious nature. For example, if a two-earth decides to throw a party, he or she will want it to be perfect in every way and will want to make sure that everyone is having a great time. The goal for these individuals is to be able to create a balance between getting their own needs met and to be present for others. They are so used to giving to others, they may not see that they need to ask for help so they can take some time to focus on themselves. Family members and friends are thrilled to see the life force enter back into their two-earth loved one once they are recharged and fulfilled. This can mean even small things, such as a much-needed walk or the time to work on a project they love or to enjoy being pampered the way they pamper others.

Two-earth individuals are very expressive and wonderful with people. Many great actors have two-earth in their charts, as do many singers with soul who sing about life and relationships.

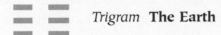 *Trigram* **The Earth**

The earth is a receptive, supportive element in nature. It has a feminine side to it—our earth is often referred to as "Mother Earth." Mother Earth invokes feelings of loving, nurturing, and warmth.

Two-earth children

Two-earth children sometimes take on others' viewpoints as their own. To help two-earth children cultivate their own opinion, listen to them without offering a viewpoint. This allows them time to figure out what they think. Two-earth children are quite sensitive, wanting to please and tending to take care of others. Consistent environments support a two-earth child in feeling safe and nurtured.

Two-earth children can appear more laid-back than other children their age and can seem more grown up. Two-earth children often choose friends who are silly and who tend to have a wild side to them. The "silly" friends bring out the lighthearted, funny side of the two-earth while the two-earth child tends to take on the grounded part of the friendship.

It is quite common for two-earth individuals to put the needs of others before their own needs because of their gracious nature.

Two-earth girls have a tendency to become little mothers to their friends and family, or they become tomboys. Two-earth boys are either a girl's best friend because they listen so well, or they become macho men. The two extremes manifest because of the nature of all yin lines in the trigrams. Everything moves to its opposite. A parent of a young two-earth girl reported that the child was destined to be a pro basketball player. She is a true tomboy who excels at the sport, yet she is also the one everyone on the team goes to for advice. One two-earth woman expressed that she spent most of her life swinging back and forth through the years from being ultra-feminine to being extremely rugged and tough. Her focus would shift.

Relationships with other people

In relationships with other people, two-earth individuals blend best with nine-fire, who support them. The two-earth individuals support six- and seven-metal as well as five- and eight-earth individuals very nicely. Two-earths tend to have a more difficult time with one-water individuals; and three- and four-tree may make them lose their focus. This does not mean that two-earth individuals can not have relationships with one-water, three-, and four-tree individuals; it simply means that they must work on the relationships a bit harder.

Combinations for two-earth individuals

Earth/Water

The earth side may create boundaries for the free-flowing one-water side of themselves. It is the same situation in nature; the earth creates the banks or shore for the water to be contained. While it is always good to have boundaries, their responsible earth nature may hold back the earth/water individual from doing things they would like to do. The grounded, strong earth nature just has to leave leeway for the free-flowing, inventive, and creative water side. It is important for earth/water people to honor both sides, and to follow their dreams. Anything that sparks creativity and enjoyment is good—painting, swimming, singing, dancing, writing, and stained glass are a few examples.

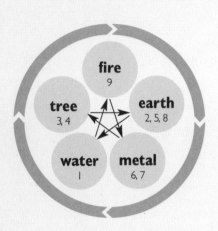

Nine Personalities

Mother Earth invokes feelings of loving, nurturing and warmth.

Earth/Tree

This combination can be a struggle sometimes because both sides have different ways of doing things. The tree is quick to move and more spontaneous than the slower-moving earth side, so there can be a push/pull within these individuals. Recognizing and honoring both sides is the key to being balanced. Both sides of their nature are equally valuable and contribute to this highly versatile personality, but the tendency is for them to second-guess themselves. The fire element creates balance in the tree/earth individuals—socializing with friends, getting out, a higher purpose, and warm colors.

Earth/Earth

These individuals are great with details and have the ability to glean insights into what is needed in the moment. They may have a hard time completing things because they continually collect information. They are usually stable and others rely on them for support. Being inspired is important for these individuals. Warm, sunlit rooms, a higher purpose, and anything that brings in the fire element helps to support them.

Earth/Metal

This combination is usually quite productive. The earth supports the metal, which results in a grounded individual. This person is very good at accomplishing what they set out to do. It is important for these individuals to be easy on themselves and take the time to let down their hair and have fun! They may have a strong personality.

Earth/Fire

These individuals have a lot to share with the world, and are great at networking and consolidating details. They may have a hard time completing things, so a secretary or helper can take all that they have created and get it out to where it needs to go. This frees them up to do what they do best. These individuals have a lot of energy, and the earth element helps to ground the energy and stabilize the focus. This is a good combination, keeping in mind that the earth is warmed by fire. Following their heart helps keep the fire element burning.

These individuals are great with details and have the ability to glean insights into what is needed in the moment.

Famous two-earth individuals

Diana Ross (2,1) pours her heart and soul into songs about life and love. Gladys Knight (2,8) of the Gladys Knight and the Pips, Nat King Cole (2,1) ("Unforgettable"), and Sonny Bono (2,2) in partnership with his bolder partner Cher (a nine-fire) ("I Got You Babe") are all two-earth performers.

Rod Stewart, Stephen Stills, Mozart, Julio Iglesias, and Patti LaBelle at first glance are so different, yet they all have the ability to write and sing songs about the ups and downs of relationships. How many times have you listened to their songs and felt really moved by the lyrics? These two-earth performers sing "soul music"—music that touches your soul.

Two-earth performers such as Jerry Lewis (2,1), Dudley Moore (2,9), Bette Davis (2,9), Marilyn Monroe (2,8), Julie Andrews (2,4), Woody Allen (2,2), Jodi Foster (2,2), Alan Alda (2,9) and Tom Selleck (2,9) have all played roles that expose life for what it is. Each of them could fit into a Woody Allen movie, which are known for their ability to reveal the human side of life with all of its frailties and strengths. His movies can make us laugh because they portray life stripped of its trappings and facades.

The Dalai Lama (2,7) is wonderful example of a two-earth who is nurturing and receptive to others. Sharing love and kindness and spirituality with others is his mission. Rosie O'Donnell (2,1), the talk show host, is another individual who loves to share kindness and love with others. Rosie is a "people person." Although she is a movie and television star, people in the audience feel connected to her, they feel like they "know" her. She is here to help others and she uses her tremendously successful talk show as a vehicle to reach out to others.

Rosie O'Donnell (2,1), the talk show host, is another individual who loves to share kindness and love with others. Rosie is a "people person."

3-Tree *the initiator*

Three-tree individuals are bold, and are often considered to be the "movers and shakers" of the world. Three-tree people are filled with new ideas and usually have many irons in the fire. Sometimes it is hard for a three-tree person to complete things because they are always going off to act on another idea. Individuals with three-tree in their charts can get bored easily if new stimuli are not pouring in. People with this energy strong in their Nine Star Ki chart are initiators and planners who are usually successful early in life. Three-tree individuals love to brainstorm. They love the challenge of coming up with new ways to do things.

It has been said that three-tree people are blunt and enjoy making a statement. They can say things that may appear shocking; this is because three-tree individuals say what is on their minds without monitoring how it may be perceived. This quality is refreshing to people who are the opposite, who have to mull things over before they speak—a lot of wasted energy to a three-tree person. When three-tree individuals are in a bad mood, their feelings can permeate the space they are in and everyone around them knows exactly how they feel. One of the greatest aspects of the three-tree personality is that you always know where you stand with them. Combined with a less bold second number/element, the bold expression may show up in less pronounced ways.

Walking in the fresh air, mountain hiking, skiing, swimming, boating, surfing, any water activities, strolling along the ocean's edge are all great ways for three-tree individuals to balance their energy and to relax. They are known for communing with the tree animals and appreciating the gifts that nature brings to us. Many three-tree people feel right at home in nature and may spend as much time outside as they can. Not all tree people love the outdoors, but it is common for three-tree individuals to need at least a few acres to go out in and plant gardens, play in the trees, manicure the grounds, and practice Zen with the groundhogs. Porches and spots where they can look out over the ponderosa, no matter how big or small, feed their soul.

It has been said that three-tree people are blunt and enjoy making a statement.

Depending on their second number this quality may show up in other ways, such as athletic endeavors. Physical exercise in their day can help to balance their energies. These individuals are usually drawn to hard, aerobic exercises. Ironically, tai chi, swimming, and other exercises that are less stressful and create more flexibility are better for supporting three-tree individuals. Stretching exercises are important to help keep them flexible. Often they hold tension in their upper body. They can experience stiff shoulders and neck.

Animals seem to love three-tree people. I have seen amazing connections between three-tree individuals and our furry friends. My dad was a perfect example of a three-tree in every way, including the love he had for animals. This next story illustrates his compassion for our four-legged friends beautifully. Dad started a ski resort with a group of his friends. One particularly cold day, he grabbed the intercom and to all of the skiers going up the mountain on the chairlift he made the following announcement. "It is extremely cold out today. There should be no animals left in the vehicles in the parking lot. If you have an animal in your car, I will give you five minutes to get to the parking lot before I let them out." Can you imagine the feeling of panic the skiers had as they ascended the mountain? I am sure their first thought was, "Who is this crazy man?" and their second thought was, "What if he really does let my animal out of the car?" That was my dad. He did what he wanted and made sure he took care of the animals.

Animals seem to love three-tree people.

 *Trigram* **Thunder**

The trigram for three-tree is thunder. Thunder comes out of the blue and is explosive; it is the same with three-tree individuals. They come on very strong, their voices can be loud, they leave their mark and move on, just as thunder does.

Three-tree children

These children tend to physically mature at an early age, due to the springtime blooming energy they possess. Three-tree children are usually very charged up or full of energy. "Full of beans" is a good term to describe these little people. They can be an explosion waiting to happen. They are always looking for the next thing to get into, the next adventure to embark on. Often they seem to be a whirlwind of activity and it can be difficult for the adults around them to keep up with them.

Challenging a point or expressing a strong opinion are common characteristics of three-tree children. Most of the time, they know what they want. My three-tree daughter loves to get a rise out of us by telling us she wants to pierce all parts of her body. Depending on the other elements in their charts, these qualities may be subtler.

Parents of tree children can do a great deal to assist their offspring by encouraging and allowing them to explore their ideas, as well as offering emotional support. Seeing that their opinion is not the only opinion can sometimes be hard for these children. Helping them see the opposite side of their opinion will only help them as they get older.

It may appear as if three-tree children do not want structure, but in essence they crave the boundaries to bounce off of. Outlets, such as athletics, allow them to express their energy and will help keep them in balance. Three-tree children need to expel their boundless energy in a safe environment.

Outdoor activities such as nature walks and camping seem to go hand in hand with three-tree children. They usually relish the outdoors and all that it offers. They are at their best when they are outside. Animals and three-tree children often have a silent bond. It is common to see a three-tree child sit down and be surrounded by animals.

Relationships with other people

Three-tree individuals blend best with one-water, who support them. The three-tree people support nine-fire individuals very nicely. Three-trees tend to have a more difficult time with two-, five-, and eight-earth individuals and six- and seven-metals can cause them to lose their focus. This does not mean that three-tree individuals cannot have relationships with six- and seven-metal individuals, and two-, five-, and eight-earth individuals, it simply means that they must work on the relationships a bit harder.

They are always looking for the next thing to get into, the next adventure to embark on.

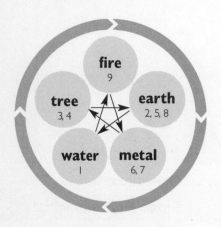

Nine Personalities

Combinations for three-tree individuals

Tree/Earth

This combination can be a struggle sometimes because both sides have a different way of doing things. The tree side is quick to move and more spontaneous than the slower-moving earth side, so there can be a push/pull within these individuals. Recognizing and honoring both sides is the key to being balanced. Both sides of their nature are equally valuable and contribute to this highly versatile personality, but they may tend to second-guess themselves. They are often decisive and fast-moving, but their emotional nature is slower to move ahead.

Tree/Metal

Metal overrides tree, which results in a strong need to honor both sides. The metal or their emotional nature may override the tree part of themselves, so it is important for them to follow their dreams and trust their decisions. The water element helps to create balance; and taking in a show, sitting by the sea, listening to peaceful music, or any activity that allows them to slow down will also help balance them.

Tree/Fire

This combination is usually fun-loving and full of beans. They may need acting classes or an outlet to express their dramatic personalities. This can be a supportive combination or it can add fuel to the fire. It may be too activating at times and they would need grounding tools to balance out the upward-expanding energy. Tai chi, sports, swing dancing, any movement-centered activities are helpful.

Tree/Water

This is a good, supportive combination—just as in nature, water supports the growth of the trees. These individuals have the ability to act on their dreams, but it's important to keep a positive outlook because they have the tendency to worry. These individuals have tremendous imagination and vision. The goal is to have balance between enjoying life, going with the flow, and being actively involved in ideas and movement that the tree element has to offer.

Tree/Tree

These people tend to get going with lots of ideas and have so many things going on at once that they need to be careful not to spread themselves too thin. They definitely are idea people. Getting recharged in nature and by the water is imperative. Grounding exercises help as well.

Famous three-tree individuals

Elvis Presley (3,3), still revered as one of the most influential performers in musical history, was a three-tree individual. He certainly ventured where no man had ever gone with his gyrating hips and soulful looks that drove teenage girls (and their parents) crazy!

Oprah Winfrey (3,3) is one who says what's on her mind. She is a pioneer of the heart and is a powerhouse who shakes up the system.

Some famous three-tree performers: Humphrey Bogart (3,3), Kirk Douglas (3,4), Lauren Hutton (3,5), Rock Hudson (3,5), Richard Burton (3,5), and Sophia Loren (3,7). All of these individuals have strong personalities that exude a presence that is bold and noticed. Not a wallflower among them!

Comedians Dick Van Dyke (3,4), Peter Sellers (3,7), and Johnny Carson (3,6) have amused us for years. They all have a tendency to overemphasize to the point of being ridiculous. One has only to call to mind Peter Sellers in any of the Pink Panther movies to laugh out loud at his ridiculous French accent and his ability to play with words.

Actors Michael Douglas and Robert DiNiro are both three-tree individuals (3,8) who have strong personalities. They play the bold mob boss or corporate head so well that it seems as though they have lived the life they are portraying. Their characters are deep individuals who have the ability to shake the audience by their deep humanitarian side (eight-earth).

Of course, there is Mick Jagger (3,9), a three-tree with nine-fire in his chart. Jagger is both a bold performer and a brilliant showman. Lisa Kudrow (1,3), who stars as Phoebe in the television sitcom *Friends,* is a free-flowing, Zen-spirited individual. Her character on *Friends* is very vocal. She enjoys telling people off in a very funny sort of way.

Oprah Winfrey (3,3) is one who says what's on her mind. She is a pioneer of the heart and is a powerhouse who shakes up the system.

4-Tree *the philosopher*

Four-tree individuals are philosophical and independent, and are very interested in higher learning. They are the eternal student. These individuals are good communicators who make wonderful teachers. They have an incredible way of telling a story or sharing an idea so that listeners can get a total picture of what they are talking about. Their communication skills are evident when they take the podium as a speaker at a planned event. They are usually eloquent in their presentation on a subject.

Four-trees usually have a message for the world and touch many people by expressing a new perspective. A good number of four-tree individuals are considered groundbreakers. They are usually recognized for what they do. This characteristic is evident in the many Nobel Prize winners who have four-tree in their charts. Many four-tree individuals are published writers. This may manifest in many other ways, such as running multitasked businesses like a production company, connecting people to where they need to be.

I often tease my sister-in-law (4,6) about being an overachiever. She is a top-class swimmer, a professional bowler, has a Ph.D. in sports psychology, has taught at the university level for three years—and she is only twenty-seven years old! (And I probably left out quite a bit about her.)

Despite the fact that four-trees can relay information to others in a learning situation such as a classroom or a seminar, it is sometimes difficult for them to express their inner feelings and emotions. Four-tree individuals often have a romantic side and a poetic nature. They tend to fall in love easily and often wear their heart on their sleeve. Love relationships seem to be their Achilles' heel. They can be going along fine—calm and cool and unruffled. As soon as they enter into a love relationship—BOOM! They do not know what happened to them. Many four-tree individuals are tender-hearted and compassionate. They enjoy imagining how others live in different parts of the world. They are

Many Nobel Prize winners have four-tree in their charts.

usually independent and most often have an urge to travel the world and explore.

It is important that four-tree individuals not take on too much at once. When they are out of balance, they can become moody and evasive. As a result of their many varied interests, they can be a bit on the eccentric side. Bathtubs to float in, fountains to listen to, things that flow, like fish tanks and small fishponds, all add the needed water element to a four-tree person's life.

Circular driveways are marvelous for keeping the flow, and so especially is a yard that is fun to work on and enjoy. Sun porches and a home that feels as if nature is peeking in through every window will give the tree person a warm, nurtured feeling. Pictures of nature or of people enjoying each other's company, and especially things that are fun and balance out responsibility, help keep the tree person feeling upbeat and able to connect with their truth. I always give one of my goofy smiling plush dogs to tree individuals to sit on their computer and smile down on them while they work.

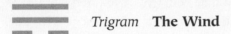 *Trigram* **The Wind**

Four-tree people are like the wind—they spread ideas and have the ability to permeate the world far and wide. The wind can be as gentle as a whisper or as wild as a gale force hurricane. The wind is invisible, but it can still be felt. This is true with the four-tree individuals. The wind is also known for scattering seeds around the earth.

Four-tree children

Four-tree children are unusually active. These children love to travel in their mind and can be quite philosophical. If given the chance, most are very interested in traveling, seeing different places and how others live.

It is very common to see four-tree children reading, writing, and physically maturing at an early age. They are so interested in the world around them, they want to find out all they can as soon as possible, and discover their independence. These children are eternal students. They truly love

They tend to fall in love easily and often wear their heart on their sleeve.

to learn and can often be heard saying, "I learn something new every day!" This does not mean that they are necessarily intellectual in a book-learning type of way, but they seem to be quite wise beyond their years as a result of their ability to take in all that is going on around them. They tend to keep a lot of their emotions and observations hidden inside; therefore, it is important for them to have a nurturing environment where they feel supported. This will help them be themselves. Depending on the second number in their chart, they may be more open with their inner emotions.

Four-tree children usually thrive around water and outdoor projects, clay, painting, drawing, and singing. Creative activities help these children to stay grounded and centered. Being able to express their ideas in a supportive environment enhances their natural ability to be terrific teachers. These children often have expressive facial and hand movements.

Four-tree children usually thrive around water and outdoor projects, clay, painting, drawing, and singing. Creative activities help these children to stay grounded and centered.

Relationships with other people

Four-tree individuals blend best with one-waters, who support them. Four-tree people support nine-fire individuals very nicely. The four-tree tends to have a more difficult time with two-, five-, and eight-earth. Six- and seven-metal can cause them to lose their focus. This does not mean that four-tree individuals cannot have relationships with six- and seven-metal individuals, and two-, five-, and eight-earth individuals; it simply means that they must work on the relationships a bit harder.

Combinations for four-tree individuals
Tree/Tree

These people tend to get lots of ideas and to have so many things going on at once that they need to be careful not to spread themselves too thin. They definitely are the idea people. Short-term goals and honoring their enthusiasm can help them prioritize their abundance of ideas. Getting recharged in nature and by the water is imperative. Grounding exercises, breathwork, and other centering activities allow them to recharge.

Tree/Fire

These people are usually fun-loving and full of beans. This can be a supportive combination or it can add fuel to the fire. A profession with high visibility and networking opportunities is optimal for tree/fire combinations. Brainstorming and community-building events can support their talents. Endurance sports, dancing, skiing, swimming, and travel keep their fire burning.

Tree/Metal

Metal overrides tree, which results in a strong need to honor both sides. For example, the skills the tree side possesses, like writing a novel with many free-flowing ideas, may be overwhelmed due to the metal side skills of honing in on what is necessary and what is not. The water element can help create balance; activities such as taking a bath, watching a show, sitting by the sea, and listening to peaceful music are all helpful. These people need to honor both sides and realize they have a lot of wonderful gifts to share with the world. So following their dreams and trusting their decisions are helpful.

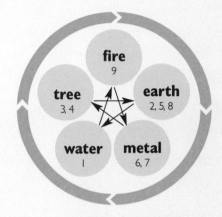

Nine Personalities

Tree/Earth

This combination can be a struggle sometimes because both sides have a different way of doing things. The tree is quick to move and more spontaneous than the slower-moving earth. So there can be a push/pull combo platter happening in these individuals. Recognizing and honoring both sides is the key to being balanced. Each side of their nature is equally valuable and contributes to this highly versatile person. Following their heart is key, as well as trusting their intuition.

Tree/Water

This is a supportive combination. Just as in nature, water supports the growth of the trees. These individuals have the ability to act on their dreams, but it's important for them to keep a positive outlook because they have the tendency to worry. They have tremendous imaginations and vision. Walks in nature and physical activities are good, with a focus on allowing the mind to rest to recharge.

Famous four-tree individuals

Carol Burnett and Barbra Streisand are both four-tree individuals (4,6). Both women can move mountains as a result of their ability to be so versatile. One minute these two performers have the audience howling with laughter, the next minute the tears are flowing. Both Burnett and Streisand have six as their second number. The six-metal side is very funny and expressive.

Paul Newman, Frank Sinatra, Paul McCartney, and Doris Day are all four-tree individuals with a romantic nature. Sinatra and McCartney both used their talents in the music arena; and Paul Newman and Doris Day have acted in a variety of romantic movies.

Harrison Ford (4,3) is a bold, philosophical performer who is a quick thinker and fast on his feet. Antonio Banderas (4,2), who starred in the remake of the old *Zorro* movie, is a romantic actor who is also considered a terrific "people person." Jennifer Aniston (4,8) who stars as Rachel in the television show *Friends*, is cast as a deeply romantic, philosophical individual.

Joan Rivers (4,4) has created a very successful business out of her entertainment success, with a jewelry and makeup line on QVC, and a funny sense of humor to boot! People love her for her ability to develop new products and to teach and share what she has learned from different cultures.

Joan Rivers (4,4) has created a very successful business out of her entertainment success, with a jewelry and makeup line on QVC, and a funny sense of humor to boot!

5-Earth *the gatherer*

Five-earth is the center of all the Nine Star Ki numbers. And five-earth individuals are often the center of attention and can do many things at once. Being of the earth element, these people are usually very grounded and do well in the public eye. You will often see five-earth individuals in public office, heading up a charitable organization, or in a political position. Five-earth individuals are recognized for their stable advice. They appear to have it all together even when they do not feel that way. They are often drawn to counseling positions, which honors their ability to give solid advice to others, although sometimes they need to search for an objective viewpoint. They are social and fun-loving and enjoy being around others. They can be the life of the party.

Five-earth individuals usually lead very eventful lives. They can be extremely charismatic, and people of all ages are attracted to their magnetic personalities. It is important that they not overextend themselves, especially in relationships. Their magnetic personalities attract many different kinds of people, some of whom become dependent on them. Five-earth individuals will take on the concerns of others because they do care about the people around them.

Five-earth people are creative problem solvers.

Five-earth people are creative problem solvers. They can look at a problem and figure out a solution that works and is unique. They are known to be very good at "coloring outside the lines." By this I mean their minds do not follow the conventional way of thinking. They have an uncanny knack of being able to look at a problem from a totally different angle than anyone else and come up with a one-of-a-kind answer.

They are very stoical and can endure hardships. They are steadfast in their perseverance of things, sometimes to the point of being obstinate. If they truly believe in something, they are like a pit bull that will not let go. They will continue until they have obtained their goal. Although five-earths can be viewed as egotistical because of their ability to be blunt, they have a very compassionate side to their nature that may not be apparent on the surface. When they are in balance, they have a tender heart that cares very deeply for those around them.

Warm, nurturing colors and fabrics are supportive for earth individuals, as are cozy furniture and a place in their home to relax and decompress after a long day. Lots of windows to let the sun beam in creates the fire energy that supports the earth individual. Earth individuals often do well to exercise regularly to keep their lymphatic system moving.

Trigram

Five-earth is represented by the center of the directions. There is no trigram associated with it. It is the balance between the two- and five-earth.

Five-earth children

Five-earth children are inquisitive and pick up "people skills" early in life. They are constantly observing the actions and words of those around them, and they can intuitively sense what works and what does not work in different situations. Nothing escapes their attention. They usually notice and carefully digest the world around them. Sometimes they ask lots of questions and sometimes they just take it all in.

One of my favorite stories about a five-earth child illustrates exactly how carefully they pay attention to the world around them. I noticed a young boy who had a marvelous gift of conversing with adults. They truly enjoyed his company, and vice versa. One day I asked him just what it was that adults enjoyed about him. He simply stated that he asked the adults questions about themselves. He showed a genuine interest in their interests! This young man learned at a very early age that people enjoy talking about themselves, especially when someone else gives them attention.

Five-earth children appear confident and on top of things. Five-earth boys will more often than not participate in several different kinds of sports. These children are usually found in leadership positions—editor of the yearbook staff, president of the club, and the like.

Five-earth children appear confident and on top of things.

Five-earth children can be very personable and they usually have a good many friends. They are often the life of the party. Five-earth individuals love to have fun. They love to entertain others by telling jokes and funny stories and they have a great knack for mimicry.

It is not unusual for five-earth children to put a great deal of pressure on themselves. These children need encouragement to be easier on themselves and to help them appreciate the goodness they possess.

Five-earth children, although extremely bright and inquisitive, may not always be the best students with the highest grades. The reason for this is their total enjoyment of the social scene, having friends, and seeing what life has to offer. Depending on what the second number is in their chart, these qualities can manifest in different ways. They can be stubborn if they feel strongly about something.

Relationships with other people

Five-earth individuals usually blend best with individuals with nine-fire in their charts. Individuals with fire in their charts support five-earth people nicely. Five-earths also do well in relationships with six- and seven-metals and the other earth numbers, two and eight. It is more difficult for five-earth individuals to be in relationships with three- and four-tree individuals and one-water individuals. This does not mean that these relationships are not possible; it just means that they take a bit more work than other relationships.

Combinations for five-earth individuals
Earth/Earth

These individuals may have a hard time completing things because they continually are in information-collecting mode. They are usually stable, and others rely on them for support. Being inspired is important for these individuals. Warm, sunlit rooms, a higher purpose, or anything that brings in the fire element helps to support them.

Nothing escapes their attention. They usually notice and carefully digest the world around them.

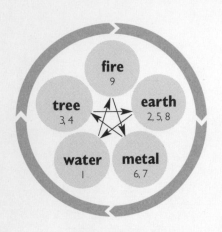

Nine Personalities

Earth/Water

The earth side may create boundaries for the free-flowing one-water side of themselves. It is the same situation in nature: The earth creates the banks or shore for the water to be contained. While it is always good to have boundaries, their responsible earth nature may hold back the earth/water individual from doing things they would like to do. The grounded, strong earth nature just has to leave leeway for the free-flowing, inventive, creative water side. It is important for earth/water people to honor both sides, to follow their dreams. Taking time to play, paint, sing, exercise, do tai chi will strengthen their connection with their inner knowing.

Earth/Tree

This combination can be a struggle sometimes because both sides have a different way of doing things. The tree is quick to move and more spontaneous than the slower-moving earth side of these individuals, so there can be a push/pull within these individuals. Recognizing and honoring both sides is the key to being balanced. Each side of this nature is equally valuable and contributes to this highly versatile personality, but these individuals tend to second-guess themselves. The fire element creates balance in the tree/earth individuals: socializing with friends, getting out, a higher purpose, warm colors.

Earth/Fire

These individuals have a lot to share with the world. They are great at networking and consolidating details. These individuals have a lot of energy and the earth element helps to ground the energy and stabilize the focus. This is a good combination, keeping in mind that the earth is warmed by fire. Following their heart helps keep the fire element burning. Activities are good that put them in the spotlight, such as heading up a club or athletic team, which keeps them in the center of things. They often have an inflence on others, so any charity work or a guidance position would be supportive for them.

Earth/Metal

Any of the earth numbers—two, five, or eight—is a very solid, complimentary combination with a metal individual. The earth numbers are very grounding. The metal/earth combination in the chart produces great teachers who are very effective and knowledgeable. The five-earth tends to want to have a good time but sometimes gets very focused and forgets to kick back. This combination can come off as authoritative because they live their life from what they have learned and want to share their knowledge.

Famous five-earth individuals

A number of famous five-earth individuals are considered to have sex appeal. Zsa Zsa Gabor (5,2), Liz Taylor (5,2), and Greta Garbo (5,4) are all actresses who exude sex appeal. Ann-Margret (5,9) and Crystal Gayle (5,9) also are considered to be very noticeable performers.

Keeping in mind that five-earth individuals are often in the public eye, it makes sense that many sportscasters and athletes have five-earth in their charts. Mark Spitz (5,9), the swimmer, and Pete Rose (5,9), the baseball player, have often been the main spokesperson for public events. Two other athletes with five-earth in their charts are Joe Dimaggio (5,2), one of the greatest baseball players of all times, and Mohammed Ali (5,9), one of the greatest boxers of all times.

Public figures with five-earth in their charts are Henry Kissinger (5,8), Thomas Jefferson (5,9), and Jesse Jackson (5,3). All three of these individuals, past and present, contributed to the growth of our country. They were not afraid to voice their opinions in their hope for a better tomorrow.

Two people considered to be geniuses in their fields were Albert Einstein (5,1) and Ludwig van Beethoven (5,1). Albert Einstein was a five-earth who revolutionized our society with his theories and inventions. Ludwig Von Beethoven was a five-earth who revolutionized our world with his brilliant gift of composing.

Two women who are very powerful entertainers, each known for her ability to captivate her audiences, are Madonna (5,1) and Celine Dion (5,1).

Two women who are very powerful entertainers, each known for her ability to captivate her audiences, are Madonna (5,1) and Celine Dion (5,1). Although Madonna and Celine Dion appear to be so different in their approach to their music and entertaining, they are both visionaries who have been able to take their talent to new heights. They are both five-earth individuals with a one-water second number in their charts.

Many singers and songwriters who have helped shape the music industry have five-earth in their charts. Bob Dylan (5,8), Bernie Taupin (Elton John's partner) (5,8), Stevie Wonder (5,8), Paul Anka (5,6), Johnny Cash (5,2), Peter Frampton (5,2), Little Richard (5,2), Art Garfunkel (5,3), Chubby Checker (5,4), Ray Charles (5,4), Dionne Warwick (5,1), and Phil Collins (5,9) have all had a hand in making the music industry what it is today.

Two actors with similar personalities are Martin Short (5,1) and Mike Myers (1,5) in the Austin Powers movies.

Two actors with similar personalities are Martin Short (5,1) and Mike Myers (1,5) in the Austin Powers movies. They are both known for their presence and their ability to play many different roles in the movies they perform in.

Jay Leno (5,9), the *Tonight Show* host, is a very influential performer who is known to be loud and boisterous, someone who is not afraid to share his views and opinions. Bill Murray (5,4) is another influential performer in the entertainment industry.

Conrad Hilton (5,1), Howard Hughes (5,1) and Aristotle Onassis (5,9) were all incredibly versatile businessmen who had five-earth in their charts. Ed McMahon, another five-earth, is a strong public personality who continues to be in the public eye with the sweepstakes and the show he cohosted for many years.

6-Metal *the leader*

Six-metal individuals are quick thinkers and very responsible types. When you hear that someone is good at "thinking on his feet," he may be a six-metal. These individuals usually are extremely quick-witted. Their minds are active, formulating new ideas; their thoughts are always swirling around. They can be extremely intense with a strong sense of responsibility. They make great investigators, terrific story-tellers, and are usually extremely creative. Other types who take more time to digest information think that the six-metal person is impulsive.

Six-metal people have a tendency to get worn out because they are so active mentally. Not only are they taking care of all that is happening now, but they tend to project their thoughts into the future and try to take care of things that may possibly happen. Different from the earth individuals, who tend to take more time to gather information before they act, six-metals jump right in and take care of things immediately, which can alarm those around them. Depending on the second number/ element in their chart, this trait can manifest in various ways.

Six-metal individuals usually have keen intuition, which is great if they trust themselves and feel comfortable with their "gut reaction" to things. These gut feelings, or first reactions, are usually right on target. Their mind can be quite powerful and may talk them out of anything ill advised; therefore, trusting their intuition is of utmost importance.

Six-metal individuals are also a lightning rod for feeling the pain and emotions of those who are around them. Being aware of this can help prevent them from taking on others' pain and heartache. It's best if they differentiate what belongs to them and what belongs to others, so they can remain centered and balanced. Six-metals usually have a great sense of humor. They are very adept at seeing the humor in everyday situations.

Six-metal individuals usually have keen intuition, which is great if they trust themselves and feel comfortable with their "gut reaction" to things.

I am a six-metal, and my friends just sit back and relax and let me do the planning when we go to a seminar or vacation together. They call me CEO Barbie (not that I look like Barbie)!

Women of this element often appear to be just "one of the guys." It is not that they are not feminine, they just have wondrous ways of saying, "These boots are made for walking." Yes, Nancy Sinatra (6,1) is a six-metal. Six-metal individuals can be foxy, but you would not want to get in the way of those boots! They are charming and quite funny, possessing a marvelous sense of humor, and they will keep you on your toes.

Exercise is important for six-metal individuals, with the focus on opening up the chest cavity and getting oxygen to the blood. Exercise that involves aerobic movement such as cycling can help keep the mind clear and the body healthy.

Exercise is important for six-metal individuals.

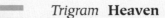 *Trigram* **Heaven**

Six-metal individuals have the trigram heaven, the creative. Energy moves down from heaven, filled with inspiration. Six-metal people need to incorporate the heaven force with the grounding energy from the earth. Chi Gung—Taoist grounding exercises—will help stabilize the strong creative energy.

Six-metal children

Six-metal children often grow up quicker than most other children do because they seem to have an uncanny ability to see what needs to be done and do it. Often they have taken care of a problem long before anyone else has seen that it was there! They can be so sensitive to the thoughts and feelings and emotions of others that this can be harmful to them. If they internalize what belongs to others, it can drain their energy and leave them quite listless and exhausted.

Their busy minds are truly an asset, but tend to stay in overdrive, so activities that are grounding and involve the body help let the mind take a rest. Tasks where they can use their creative ability work too. Drawing, making ornaments, baskets, rugs, and knitting all are things that require creative juices and help ground six-metals.

A home life where hugs are offered freely often can help slow down these six-metal children and make them feel safe. These children usually thrive with lots of physical warmth and caring. If a six-metal has a parent who is hard on her, she can become self-critical. Singing is great for these children because it stimulates the lungs, which can be where the metal person may hold on to self-doubt or judgment. Using their creativity helps them connect with their heart's desire.

Warm, cozy colors have a warming nurturing effect on metal people. A comfy chair in a special place in the house can help the six-metal child chill out and decompress. Many six-metal people love the idea of a game room or a place to turn the phone off and paint, exercise, or dance. Taking time out isn't what six-metals do best, so it may be an effort but well worth it. Warm, soft colors that call you will calm the nervous system; children benefit from this especially in their bedroom. The kitchen is a place that usually holds magic where people gather and share. Six-metal individuals sometimes are too on the move to enjoy this or to realize that the food we eat is our fuel. Making the kitchen a place that has joyful, fun things around will help the six-metal child feel good in the kitchen.

Relationships with other people

Six-metal individuals blend best with two-, five-, and eight-earth and seven-metal, who support them. Six-metals support one-waters very nicely. Six-metals tend to have a more difficult time with three- and four-tree individuals. Nine-fires may make them lose their focus. This does not mean that six-metal individuals cannot have relationships with three- and four-tree, and nine-fire individuals; it simply means that they must work on the relationships a bit harder.

Combinations for six-metal individuals
Metal/Metal

They are usually very active and creative, and tend to give out life force energy to others because they see where others need help. These people need to do restorative exercise to regain their energy and ground. They need to nurture themselves. Most six-metals have a great sense of

Six-metal children often grow up quicker than most other children do because they seem to have an uncanny ability to see what needs to be done and do it.

humor. They need to be easy on themselves, and to be careful not to be self-critical.

Metal/Fire

This combo can be overwhelming because the fire element tends to scatter the metal element. A metal combined with a nine-fire can be an overwhelming combination. Meditative exercises are good to help ground this individual. It is important to honor both the metal and fire sides of the personality. The fire side is expressive and in the now, the metal is focused and more future oriented. Honoring both sides of their nature is key; both aspects have a lot of amazing gifts to share with the world. Taking time to enjoy being home and relaxing can keep them centered. They can take on too much, so any way to ground and get clarity to what actually will serve their overall goal is helpful.

Metal/Tree

Metal overrides tree, which results in a strong need to honor both sides. The water element can help create balance—things like taking a bath, taking in a show, sitting by the sea, listening to peaceful music are all helpful. These people need to honor both sides and realize they have a lot of wonderful gifts to share with the world. So following their dreams and trusting their decisions is key. They need to take time to smell the flowers, play with the dog, go out for dinner—anything that can help them not to get too scattered and take on too much.

Metal/Earth

This combination is usually quite supportive and productive. The earth supports the metal, which results in a grounded individual. These people are very good at accomplishing what they set out to do. It is important that they be easy on themselves and take the time to let down their hair and have fun! They will appear confident even when they don't feel that way at all. Leadership positions, organizing groups, and teaching all can be supportive for these individuals. Exercise will keep their mind clear.

Nine Personalities

Metal/Water

This is a supportive combination. Metal supports water. The water can help decompress the active, moving metal energy. The metal is a strong creative base for the visionary quality in the water nature. These individuals can be serious, so there is a need to have fun and lift the energy by doing new things and enjoying others' company. Writing, inventing, and sharing their ideas with the world will keep their creativity alive.

Famous six-metal individuals

Famous six-metal individuals include a number of "these boots are made for walking" ladies. Nancy Sinatra (6,1), Raquel Welch (6,8), Sharon Stone (6,4), Morgan Fairchild (6,3), Kathleen Turner (6,1), Meryl Streep (6,1), Sissy Spacek (6,4), Faye Dunaway (6,3), Whoopie Goldberg (6,5), Toni Braxton (6,7), and Jamie Lee Curtis (6,5) are all very well known for their incredible abilities to act in all situations. Julia Roberts (6,6) is another six-metal who is known for her quick wit and charm. She, too, wore boots in *Pretty Woman!*

It is interesting to note the number of Nobel Prize winners who have six-metal as their first or second numbers: Menachem Begin (6,7), Wendel Stanley (6,7), Herman Hesse (4,6) and Ernest Hemingway (2,6), to name a few.

The news industry is dominated by six-metal individuals: Barbara Walters (6,7), Dan Rather (6,6), Ted Koppel (6,5), Tom Brokaw (6,5), Morley Safer (6,5), Andy Rooney (1,6), Douglas Edwards (3,6), and Walter Cronkite (3,6).

One of the qualities that six-metals possess is a great sense of humor. This is evident in the works of *Peanuts* creator Charles Schulz (6,5), Dr. Seuss (6,5) of *The Cat in the Hat* fame, and Walt Kelly (6,5), the creator of the comic character Pogo. Each of these six-metals shows life in a humorous light to get a point across.

One of the qualities that six-metals possess is a great sense of humor. This is evident in the works of Peanuts *creator Charles Schulz (6,5), Dr. Seuss (6,5) of* The Cat in the Hat *fame, and Walt Kelly (6,5), the creator of the comic character Pogo.*

7-Metal *the problem solver*

Seven-metal individuals typically come with a "how to" manual on how life operates. These individuals have the ability to see how things work. They usually are organized and focused and love to figure things out. Problem solving is one of their great strengths. Seven-metal individuals do well in any occupation that encourages them to be prepared and organized. Seven-metals also make good teachers because they are resourceful and can simplify lessons and explain them at the level of the students they are teaching.

My brother, a seven-metal, created a miniature chairlift in his room when he was young, for his Stief Bears to ride up and around the room! He conceived the idea and put all of the elements together to make the chairlift work. He also invented a boat that had a motor in the back, which he could steer from the front with pull cords. He has the ability to see how things work and can put them together to meet his specifications.

Often individuals with seven-metal in their charts are "systems" people. They know how to work in the system and they enjoy figuring out a way to "beat the system." These people are the ones who write the manuals on how systems operate. Not all seven-metals have systems as their interest; but more often than not, wherever their interests lie they have a method to make it work for them. One seven-metal I know used his systems skills to direct many individuals to work as a whole; another fellow used these skills to build race cars and bet at the horse races.

This quality may show up in simpler ways, such as picking things up easily. Two seven-metal women I know use their talents in businesses that take an enormous amount of understanding of how things go together. One runs a hardware store and gives advice on building and how things go together, to get her customers the results they are looking for. The other is a very successful caterer; she has to coordinate many projects at a time, as well as put together combinations of foods that will suit the needs of her clients. Both women are highly systematic in their work.

Problem solving is one of their great strengths.

Seven-metal individuals make natural race car drivers. They can be fascinated with gadgets, and they have a knack for making complex things simple. Seven-metals are the ones who go to the moon, such as Neil Armstrong (7,3), or figure out a mystery. They can be seen in films jumping over canyons, taking apart bombs, and rescuing women and children from impossible situations. Yes, you can sometimes see a little James Bond in them. Throughout it all, they keep their wits about them. They are very cool, calm, and collected.

They are incredibly intuitive and are usually right when they go with their gut feeling. Seven-metals are similar to six-metal individuals with their keen intuition, yet they must take care to not overanalyze situations. Seven-metal individuals are often considered psychic because of their uncanny ability to sense others' thoughts. Some will exhibit more of their day-to-day nature, and others will show more of their emotional nature, and some are a balance of the two. So where the seven-metal falls in the chart will influence how you see them express themselves.

Seven-metal individuals can often appear overpowering because they have no qualms about voicing their opinion. They have an attitude of "If it works for me, it will work for you." It is challenging for seven-metals to see that people are different and walk to the beat of their own drummer.

Warm, rich fabrics, natural fibers, and poofy furniture are supportive for these people. Seven-metal people do well to have music playing, fun friends over to enjoy their home, and food cooking in the kitchen. Satisfying the senses is important for them. If a seven-metal isn't reminded to kick back he may forget to take his head out of mental activities. Warm wall colors help them relax. A hot tub or whirlpool might be the perfect relaxing tool. They love to kick back and relax but are usually seen on the go, putting things together or creating new ways to do things.

On a psychological level, emphasize comfort and coziness. Taking walks by a river or stream, and water skiing, boating, sailing, any water activities help balance out and quench the seven-metals' need to be active. Taking time out to watch comedies with friends and laugh out loud supports them. Get the guitar out and play a tune for friends,

On a psychological level, emphasize comfort and coziness.

spend more time with others, especially children. They need permission to be vulnerable and to express deep feelings.

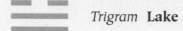 *Trigram* **Lake**

Their trigram in the *I Ching* is the Lake. It is calm on the surface but a great deal of churning is going on beneath the surface.

Seven-metal children

It is not unusual for seven-metal children to have very little interest in school. They are too busy putting their curiosity to use by building the fastest go-cart in the neighborhood or figuring out how to make the remote control plane fly faster! Book learning and listening to the teacher often do not stimulate seven-metal children to learn. One mom of a seven-metal child was quite upset to find out that he was failing in school. His teachers all expressed great concern over him because he was so bright and quite capable; he was just not performing up to the school's expectations. This child grew up to be a multimillionaire. He knew that school was not meeting his needs, yet he was able to translate his ability to put things together in the right environment to a successful business career.

It is very important that these children have a home life that is warm and nurturing. It is easy for them to insulate themselves from the world, therefore it is extremely important that they receive lots of hugs and physical support from their parents. Keep praising these children, and they will thrive. If they are not encouraged and their efforts are belittled, they may grow up frustrated and turn to drugs and alcohol to vent their unhappiness.

Seven-metal children are the ones who may grow up being like James Bond in the adventure thrillers. It is important that they have Tinkertoys and LEGO blocks around to build their fantasy cars and planes. The sunglasses and the fancy suits can come later.

Keep praising these children, and they will thrive.

Relationships with other people

Seven-metal individuals blend best with two-, five-, and eight-earth and six-metals, who support them. The seven-metal individuals support one-water individuals very nicely. Seven-metals tend to have a more difficult time with three- and four-tree individuals. Nine fire can override them. This does not mean that seven-metal individuals cannot have relationships with nine-fire, and three- and four-tree individuals; it simply means they must work on the relationships a bit harder.

Combinations for seven-metal individuals
Metal/Water

This is a supportive combination. Metal supports water. The water can help decompress the active, moving metal energy. The metal is a strong creative base for the visionary quality in the water nature. These individuals can be serious, so there is a need to have fun and lift the energy by doing new things and enjoying others' company. Writing, inventing, and sharing their ideas with the world will keep their creativity alive.

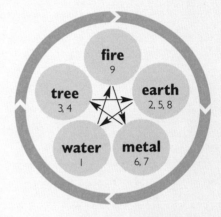

Nine Personalities

Metal/Tree

Metal overrides tree, which results in a strong need to honor both sides of the nature. They may tend to override their emotional needs (metal overides tree), realizing the metal nature will look at things differently than the tree nature. The water element can help create balance—things like taking a bath, taking in a show, sitting by the sea, listening to peaceful music are all helpful. These people need to honor both sides and realize they have a lot of wonderful gifts to share with the world—to follow their dreams and trust their decisions.

Metal/Fire

This combo can be overwhelming because the fire element tends to scatter the metal element. A metal with a nine-fire can be an overwhelming combination. Meditative exercises are good to help ground this individual. It is important to honor both the metal and fire sides of the personality. The fire side is expressive and in the now; the metal is focused and more future-oriented. Honoring both sides of their nature is key: Both aspects have a lot of amazing gifts to share with the world. It is although a constant balancing act between the expansive fire element and the more focused channeled metal element.

Metal/Earth

Any of the earth numbers—two, five, or eight—are a solid complement to a seven-metal individual. The earth numbers are very grounding. Combined with the eight-earth emotional nature, their focus may be more inward as opposed to the seven-metal/five-earth or two-earth combinations. Simplifying and organizing, researching usually come as a second nature for these individuals.

Metal/Metal

The double metal nature is direct, self-confident and hardworking. They are good organizers. They need a home to relax in and a good support system. The water element helps them to unwind. Water activities are good, including swimming or even sitting by a stream. Creative, free-flowing activities such as dance and artistic endeavors keep them flowing. They are very intuitive. It is important for them to have a rich social life.

Famous seven-metal individuals

Of course, Sean Connery (7,2) is a seven-metal. The actor epitomizes the James Bond character he has played in so many movies: jumping canyons with the best of them, dismantling bombs, and always showing up where others would have thought it impossible! Steve McQueen (7,7), Clint Eastwood (7,5), Gene Hackman (7,6), Cary Grant (7,6), and Robert Wagner (7,8) all have the "dark glasses," a certain kind of attitude coupled with an uncanny sense of humor that makes you love them. All of these actors have portrayed the same type of character: one who figures out the most amazing puzzle while remaining calm in the face of inevitable chaos.

Other seven-metal individuals: Lawrence (Bubbles) Welk (7,1), beloved orchestra leader; Bob Hope (7,5) and Jack Benny (7,8), two funny comedians.

Water activities are good, including swimming or even sitting by a stream.

George Washington (7,8), Ulysses S. Grant (7,6), and Theodore Roosevelt (7,9) were all leaders of our country. They served as presidents of the United States and as leaders of armies during wartime.

Julia Childs (7,2), the cooking diva, always entertains her watchers by adding ingredients to her creations using a dramatic flair.

Seven-metal individuals usually appreciate music and have the ability to be versatile. Janet Jackson (7,5) is a seven-metal who is very influential in the music world. She is focused, and when she believes in a cause, she throws her support in to make a difference.

Lily Tomlin (7,2) is a talented performer who is very funny and enjoyable to watch because she gives you the feeling you are watching many people at once. She is wonderfully versatile in her ability to create different personas.

Seven-metal individuals usually appreciate music.

8-Earth *the contemplator*

Eight-earth individuals are deep-thinking and introspective. They have an interesting combination of character traits: On the one hand, they are soulful and deeply contemplative. On the other, they can be competitive and highly motivated individuals. Eight-earth individuals are gentle on the outside, but they have a strong, solid constitution. They tend to sit back and observe all that is happening around them. They take it all in, understanding completely the dynamics of the situation.

Eight-earth individuals often have a strong sense about preserving the earth in some way or another. They usually care deeply and find themselves in professions that put that quality to use. One of my clients who is an eight-earth is a physician who is very intuitive and deeply concerned about the welfare of her patients. This doctor shared with me the fact that before she went to medical school, she had been enrolled in veterinary school. She cared so deeply for the animals in the lab that she could not bear the thought of them being cut open to study. She spent so much time switching out of classes that studied animals in inhumane ways, she ended up quitting vet school. She decided to go to medical school and use her skills in caring for people.

Individuals with eight-earth in their chart often grow up feeling that no one really understands them. If an eight-earth is not pressured to be more outgoing, he or she will be a good friend and support to others in life. Many eight-earth individuals love to have their space and won't easily tell you what is on their mind. Allow them to offer their thoughts to you in their own time. They are meditative, deep-thinking individuals who are always checking in with themselves.

Eight-earth individuals are usually on a mission. This is illustrated by some of the examples of famous people who have eight-earth in their charts. Whether they are trying to help humanity through religion, through the written word, through the medium of painting, or on the big screen, eight-earth individuals have the unique ability to touch another

Eight-earth individuals are usually on a mission.

human being in their own special way. They definitely leave an impression and are remembered for what they have done. Jami Lin (8,8), a Feng Shui consultant, is a woman on a mission. She took on the amazing task of bringing forty consultants together in one book, *A Feng Shui Anthology*. Her life is about changing the world.

I received a call from a client (8,2) who was unhappy about his almost completed, newly constructed home. He was confused by his mixed feelings about the finished dwelling. His Nine Star Ki numbers reflected the two opposite sets of feelings he was having. His first number, eight-earth, the day-to-day number, reflected his practical nature, which was telling him that he must stay within the original budget. His second number, two-earth, the emotional number, was challenging his thoughts about the budget. It was forcing him to think about the entertaining he enjoyed and the comforts that came along with having friends over to share an evening of food and fun.

His emotional side wanted to include large, luxurious bathrooms, while the actual size of the structure reflected his practical side. The physical layout of the house would not allow for the luxuries that he desired. The house did not have the flow to it that would make him feel comfortable and supported.

This man was feeling very frustrated with his options. When we looked at his scenario together, it was a pattern that had been haunting him all his life. He realized that he would continually berate himself for thinking about make a purchase that seemed frivolous, not in the least bit practical. As a result, he was constantly bouncing back and forth on decisions that fell in the nonpractical category. He discovered that he was always compromising and choosing only the things that he felt were practical. He was never happy or completely satisfied with his decision. By not indulging the emotional side of his personality, by not purchasing something that was not practical, he was actually doing himself an injustice. He finally saw that he could honor the emotional side of his personality and make a choice to purchase something a bit more extravagant and that would help to bring about a balance in his life.

If an eight-earth is not pressured to be more outgoing, he or she will be a good friend and support to others in life.

Trigram **Mountain**

Eight-earth is associated with the mountain trigram, which represents deep inner knowing. On the inside it is stable. Through inner exploration, change and transformation occur on the outside.

Eight-earth children

Eight-earth children have a very deep, introspective side. If they feel secure in their environment, they will be comfortable sharing their thoughts and feelings. If they are pushed and asked constantly to share what is on their mind, they will tighten up like a clam and keep it all inside.

It is very important for them to have a space in their home that they can call their own. They "need their own space" to cocoon and be alone with their thoughts. (This is true for these individuals as they grow to adulthood.) These souls can be very private.

Eight-earth children can often be very serious and have such a true concern for others around them that they can often forget to have fun. It is helpful to find an outlet for these children that will get them laughing and having fun. Sunlit rooms and bright, fiery colors can also nurture these contemplative souls. Friends are important for these children; being able to play and do physical activities that involve others helps create balance for them.

A friend (2,8) of my daughter constantly keeps an eye on who in the class is littering and recycling. She is a calm and steady presence, which the other children find stabilizing. My son Patrick is a (5,8). The five-earth side of him allows him to enjoy the social scene, but the eight-earth side runs extremely deep. He feels things very intensely and he has a great concern for others' well-being. Often his concerns are on a global level. The eight-earth people are not "pussyfooting" around—they mean business! Their soulful nature can manifest in many different ways, and if the fire or tree element is present in the chart, their tendency will be to be much more expressive.

Sunlit rooms and bright, fiery colors can also nurture these contemplative souls. Friends are important for these children.

Relationships with other people

Earth individuals blend best with nine-fire, who support them. The eight-earth individuals support six- and seven-metal individuals very nicely. Eight-earths tend to have a more difficult time with one-water individuals; three- and four-trees can make them lose their focus. This does not mean that eight-earth individuals cannot have relationships with one-water, and three- and four-tree individuals; it simply means that they may have to work on the relationships a bit harder.

Combinations for eight-earth individuals

Earth/Earth

These individuals are great with details and have the ability to glean insights into what is needed in the moment. They may have a hard time completing things because they continually are collecting information. They are usually stable, and others rely on them for support. Being inspired is important for these individuals. They benefit from warm, sun-lit rooms, a higher purpose—anything that brings in the fire element helps to support them.

Earth/Fire

These individuals have a lot to share with the world; they are often great at networking and consolidating details. They have a lot of energy, and the earth element helps to ground the energy and stabilize their focus. These individuals have a big heart and would be great at leading a charity group or fundraising event.

Earth/Water

The earth side may create boundaries for the free-flowing one-water side of themselves. It is the same in nature: The earth creates the banks or shore for the water to be contained. While it is always good to have boundaries, their responsible earth nature may hold back the earth/water individual from doing things they would like to do. The grounded, strong earth nature just has to leave leeway for the free-flowing, inventive, creative water side. These individuals usually have healing gifts and influence how others see spiritual issues.

Nine Personalities

Earth/Tree

This combination can be a struggle sometimes, because both sides have a different way of doing things. The tree is quick to move and more spontaneous than the slower-moving earth, so there can be a push/pull within these individuals. Recognizing and honoring both sides is the key to being balanced. Both sides of their nature are equally valuable and contribute to this highly versatile personality, but the tendency is for them to second-guess themselves. The fire element creates balance in tree/earth individuals—socializing with friends, getting out, a higher purpose, warm colors.

Earth/Metal

Any of the earth numbers—two, five, or eight—is a very solid, complementary combination with a metal individual. The earth numbers are very grounding. The seven-metal/earth (7,8) combination in the chart produces great teachers who are very effective, although these individuals may be a bit too serious. It is important for them to have fun and enjoy themselves.

Famous eight-earth individuals

Many successful writers have eight-earth in their charts.

It is not surprising that many successful writers have eight-earth in their charts. They have such a depth of feeling to them that they want to share with others. Different writers share this intensity in different ways. Elton John (8,1) and Emmy Lou Harris (8,1) are both visionaries and soulful songwriters. You can *feel* the intensity of the emotions they sing about. Steven Spielberg (8,1) is an intense writer/director who wants to have an impact on the world. John Steinbeck (8,2), Charles Dickens (8,2), and Stephen King (8,4) are all eight-earth types who have written about society in ways that touch us. Each has a different style but each gives the reader food for thought. Their writings force the reader to stop and think about the subject at hand.

Pope John Paul II (8,8) is a perfect example of an eight-earth individual who wants to help alleviate suffering and hardship in the world. Lucille Ball (6,8), the beloved comedienne who had us in tears of laughter and tears of sorrow, used the eight-earth in her chart to help convey the intensity of her emotions.

9-Fire *the star*

The star of the show is typically a nine-fire individual. When you think of fire, you think of the flames flickering all around, spreading light and warmth to all who are around them. That is the personality of individuals with nine-fire in their chart. They are usually very warm, social, and naturally gregarious, with very big hearts. Nine-fire individuals love to shine.

It is important to tend a fire, to feed it in order for the flames to continue dancing and the warmth of the flames to continue to spread. It is the same with nine-fire individuals. They have a tremendous need to be supported. If they are not supported, they can flicker, dim, and eventually burn out. Occasionally you will find a shy nine-fire who is a wallflower, but more likely, the nine-fire secretly or overtly wants to be the center of attention. If nine-fire individuals are not encouraged to be their naturally wild, exotic, highly visible self, their light may be dimmed and their true self hidden in their attempt to be like those around them.

It is important that nine-fire individuals be clear about their boundaries. Without boundaries, they can really find themselves unsure of where they end and someone else begins. Because their energy field is so expansive, having a home that has an expansive feel is important. Nine-fires have a natural tendency to "push the envelope," or continue to challenge the boundaries they are faced with in life. They live in the moment. As a result, it is sometimes difficult for these individuals to commit to a steady relationship with a member of the opposite sex.

Have you ever heard someone say they have a friend who could sell air-conditioning to an Eskimo in an igloo in December? They are probably referring to a nine-fire individual. Nine-fires are naturals at convincing others about what they need. They could truly sell a dime for a quarter.

Getting recognition for their efforts is extremely important for nine-fire individuals. They are happy to do the work, but they would like to be recognized for it.

Occasionally you will find a shy nine-fire who is a wallflower.

Nine-fire individuals typically at some time in their life strive to be in tune with their spirituality and need to feel connected to their higher purpose in life. Depending on the other elements in the chart, the fire nature can express itself in many different ways.

Open windows that draw in natural sunlight help to recharge the nine-fire. Outdoor pictures, plants, earthy tile floors, greens, and warm colors all nurture nine-fires. If a nine-fire is true to his nature and likes to entertain, a festive kitchen and dining area, a cozy living room, help create balance for him. Decorating usually come easily for a nine-fire—even the males have an art for seeing where things go. One nine-fire male told me he couldn't do anything with his house; but the art of display expressed itself through his profession—he was amazing at graphic design. Adding fresh flowers weekly gives an uplifting, cheery, colorful feel. A greenhouse or sun porch can be a great place to hang out and have fun. Too much red or green can be overly stimulating, as can too much wood, such as wood floors, ceilings, walls, and furniture all in one room.

Trigram **Fire**

The Fire trigram represents social interaction, spreading of ideas, networking, inspiration, and being able to be recognized for who you are. It can be about being in the public eye. It is the warmth of the sun and the passion that inspires us. It is expanding, illuminating, and expressive.

Nine-fire children

Often parents will try to calm their nine-fire children down or keep them from being overly active. This is a constant challenge for parents and teachers alike. There is a fine line between helping to settle their energy down and putting out their fire. Their energy field can be so expansive that it is overwhelming for others at times. Finding an outlet for their natural fire personality to express itself, such as acting classes, dancing—any activity that will keep them in the spotlight—will suit the fire child just perfectly. Like adults who have nine-fire in their charts, these children love the visibility that comes with entertaining. They can be captivating and warmhearted. These traits will be less visible if they have a metal or earth element as their second number. A (9,7) who was

Open windows that draw in natural sunlight help to recharge the nine-fire. Outdoor pictures, plants, earthy tile floors, greens, and warm colors all nurture nine-fires.

very quiet as a child said her nine-fire would surface when she would go to the hospital to visit her mom at work. She'd sneak into the patients' rooms and tell them stories and entertain them for hours.

Parents of a nine-fire child can help their naturally active and energetic child with gentle forms of structure and orderly discipline. Again, if nine-fires have an earth element in their chart, they tend to be more contained.

Our daughter is a three, nine (3,9). My husband and I were in a clothing store and a stranger approached us and asked our daughter to try on clothes that might fit her granddaughter. Susie jumped at the chance to model the outfit. She was delighted not only to model several outfits, but also to give her suggestions on appropriate choices! When she was five she was offered modeling jobs, which she was too shy to take. Now she looks back and cannot believe she didn't jump on it. Some times it takes just the right environment to bring the gregarious Mick Jagger (3,9) side out of a nine-fire personality.

Some clients shared with me how they always encouraged their daughter, who was an actress, to shine, knowing she was a star. The daughter never had any reservations about being in the spotlight; in fact, she enjoyed it. As an adult, this young woman is very confident, speaks her truth, and has a great many acting jobs offered to her.

Another nine-fire child I know was constantly held under her parents' thumb. Instead of her fiery personality being allowed to burn brightly, she had to keep it all cooped up inside. She had a very shy nature as she grew up and she would become extremely silly only in front of those who would cheer her on and support her without laughing at her. She put a great deal of her energy into other people, making sure their needs were met; yet she ignored her own needs. It took her a long time to balance her life out. I see these two scenarios play out all the time in my Feng Shui practice. The theme here is for them to be themselves and follow their life's path.

When nine-fire individuals are out of balance, their thoughts become scattered and they can become hyperactive and overly dramatic. It's as if they are going in too many directions. When things are not in sync for

There is a fine line between helping to settle their energy down and putting out their fire.

nine-fires, it is important for them to focus their energy. When they are in balance, nine-fire individuals are full of love and compassion and are exciting to be around. People are attracted to their magnetic personality and inner warmth and love to be close to them.

Relationships with other people

Nine-fire individuals blend best with three- and four-trees, who support them. The nine-fire individuals support two-, five-, and eight-earth individuals very nicely. Nine-fire individuals tend to have a more difficult time with six- and seven-metal individuals; one-waters may make them lose their focus. This does not mean that nine-fire individuals cannot have relationships with one-water or six and seven-metal individuals; it simply means that they must work on the relationships a bit harder.

Combinations for nine-fire individuals

Fire/Fire

This person feels as if they have a world to explore—so let's get to it. They can be social butterflies if they were encouraged in childhood to be themselves. Being in the limelight comes easy, although these individuals can have a shy side. They are most often tenderhearted. These individuals usually have strong personalities and may intimidate others even though that is not their intention. Fire individuals have expansive energy fields and need enough space to move in; for example, a small apartment most likely would drive them crazy. They can appear hotheaded.

Fire/Tree

The tree element supports the fire, so walks in nature would be recharging. Jobs where people can totally be themselves and be appreciated for their talents support them. If they are not fulfilled and don't have a higher purpose these individuals will slowly burn out and get depressed. Being appreciated helps.

Fire/Earth

These individuals have a lot to share with the world. They are great at networking and consolidating details. These individuals have a lot of energy, and the earth element helps to ground the energy and stabilize

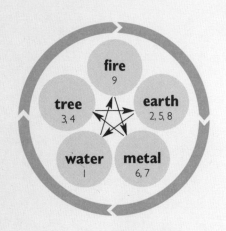

Nine Personalities

the focus. This is a good combination, keeping in mind that the earth is warmed by fire. These individuals most often exude confidence and have a strong viewpoint, making them perfect for a job such as a talk show host or a sportscaster.

Fire/Metal

This combo can be overwhelming because the fire element tends to scatter the metal element. A metal with a nine-fire can be an overwhelming combination. Meditative exercises are good to help ground this individual. It is important to honor both the metal and fire sides of the personality. The fire side is expressive and in the now; the metal is focused and more future-oriented. Honoring both sides of their nature is key; both aspects have a lot of amazing gifts to share with the world, although it is a constant balancing act between the expansive fire element and the more focused, channeled metal element. One fire/metal man used his skills to negotiate and work on contracts. Bill Gates is a good example of high visibility combined with a good business sense.

Fire/Water

Think of the properties in nature: Water can be used to put out fire, yet it can make a grease fire spread. The fire side of this combination must fight hard to shine. These individuals may appear like two different people, very deep one minute, more superficial the next, which can make it hard to read their intention. The tree element helps to bridge these opposite sides, so activities such as walking and hiking in a beautiful place will bring this combination into balance. It usually is rejuvenating for one-water/nine-fire to get outside in nature—it helps them manifest new ideas. It would be helpful for these people to honor both sides of themselves. Having the limelight in some way and getting recognition for their talents are helpful. The fire side may wilt away if they are unable to be true to their expressive, entertaining side. Having a higher purpose in life also helps stabilize them.

Famous nine-fire individuals

Highly visible women such as Cher (9,2), Candice Bergen (9,2), Shirley Temple (9,3), Liza Minnelli (9,4), Jane Fonda (3,9), and Suzanne

When they are in BALANCE, *nine-fire individuals are full of love and compassion and are exciting to be around.*

Sommers (9,1) are all nine-fire individuals. Each of them is a performer with tremendous amounts of energy who truly enjoys having the glow of the spotlight surround them. Marie Antoinette (9,6) and Mae West (9,8) also had fiery personalities that they were famous for.

Two extremely talented, versatile actors, Dustin Hoffman (9,8) and Robert Redford (9,8), ironically have the same first two numbers. They have a deep introspective middle-earth nature combined with a highly visible "knock 'em dead" nature.

Mother Teresa was a nine-fire. When one thinks of this tiny lady, it is not her diminutive stature that comes to mind, but her huge heart that emanated a warm, nurturing presence in the world.

Bill Cosby (9,9) is a wonderful example of a warmhearted performer who has nine-fire in his chart.

Mother Teresa was a nine-fire.

Calista Flockhart (9,5), the main character in the television show *Ally McBeal,* has been credited by her producer as the reason the show is so successful. He stated at an awards presentation that all she has to do is show up and the dialogue comes naturally. Courtney Cox (9,1), a television actress in the show *Friends,* plays a very visible character whose personality ranges from one extreme to the other.

Bill Gates (9,6) has taken advantage of the qualities of the two elements in his chart. He is highly visible and has incredible networking ability (nine-fire), and he would also have to be extremely focused to have created what he has. His success is a result of his ability to create a company that re-creates itself on a regular basis.

Books

■ *The Book of Changes and the Unchanging Truth*
    by Hua-Ching Ni.
    Published by Seven Star Communications
    My favorite book on the I Ching.

■ *Nine-Star Ki: Your Astrological Companion to Feng Shui*
    by Bob Sachs.
    Published by Element Books, Ltd. and
    distributed by Putnam-Penguin.
    Website: ninestarki.net
    Email: diamond.way.ayurveda@thegrid.net

■ *The Essence of Feng Shui*
    by my friend and colleague, Jami Lin.
    Published by Hay House, Inc.
    A great uplifting book on fragrance
    and Feng Shui.

■ *Feng Shui Made Easy*
    by William Spear.
    Published by Harper of San Francisco.
    A great beginner's book.

■ *Food and Healing*
    by Annemarie Colbin.
    Published by Ballantine Books.
    The best and most balanced book on food
    energetics I have ever read.

■ *Awaken Healing Light of the Tao*
    by Mantak & Maneewan Chia.
    Available through International Healing Tao.
    Very detailed and thorough introduction
    to Taoism.

Resources

■ *Hands on Design*
Amazing pottery, sinks, whimsical plates, mugs, candelabras, animal characters—all in gorgeous Feng Shui colors. Can be seen on my web site or call Louise McConnell at (804) 979-0333.

■ *Doug's Tubs*
Beautiful fixtures, waterfall spouts, as well as good deals on tubs, and more. www.dougstubs.com; (800) 991-2284.

■ *William McDonough and Partners*
Architecture firm focuses on the consequences of design across all scales, from the molecular to the master plan. Amazing design implemented all around the globe. www.mcdonough.com; (804) 979-1111.

■ *Sherwin-Williams Harmony paint*
A less toxic, low-VOC paint, friendly to the lung, with nice color choice. Many health-care facilities use this paint. Glidden 2000 and Benjamin Moore ECO are available as well.

■ *Sylvania*
Makes a soft pink bulb for three-way and regular lamps. This marvelous lighting is easy on the eyes and nervous system. Great for light deprivation disorders, this bulb is much warmer than average. It doesn't appear pink, but rather puts out a warm glow that's nice for the complexion. Available at most home stores.

■ *QVC*
Whether on-line or through the shopping channel, this is a nice resource for torchier lamps. Its many choices of lamps sending light up toward the ceiling includes Old Mission styles.

■ *Ferguson Gallery*
A variety of wonderful choices of lighting fixtures and creative designs. They have showrooms all over the U.S. www.ferguson.com.

New World Library
is dedicated to publishing books
and cassettes that inspire
and challenge us to improve the quality
of our lives and our world.
Our books and cassettes are available
at bookstores everywhere.
For a complete catalog, contact:

New World Library
14 Pamaron Way
Novato, California 94949
Phone: (415) 884-2100
Fax: (415) 884-2199
Or call toll free: (800) 972-6657
Catalog requests: Ext. 50
Ordering: Ext. 52
E-mail: escort@nwlib.com
newworldlibrary.com